THE GRINNING GARDENER'S HANDBOOK VOLUME 1

A COMPREHENSIVE GUIDE TO GROWING AMAZING ORGANIC FRUITS AND VEGETABLES IN DIFFERENT CLIMATES AND SEASONS

KENT JAMESON

Copyright © 2024 by Kent Jameson

All rights reserved. No part of this book may be reproduced, distributed, or transmitted in any form or by any means, including photocopying, recording, or other electronic or mechanical methods, without the prior written permission of the publisher, except in the case of brief quotations embodied in critical reviews and certain other noncommercial uses permitted by copyright law. For permission requests, contact the publisher at the address below.

Disclaimer Notice:

Please note the information contained within this document is for educational and entertainment purposes only. All effort has been expended to present accurate, up-to-date, and reliable, complete information. No warranties of any kind are declared or implied. Readers acknowledge that the author is not engaging in the rendering of legal, financial, medical or professional advice. The content within this book has been derived from various sources. Please consult a licensed professional before attempting any techniques outlined in this book.

By reading this document, the reader agrees that under no circumstances is the author responsible for any losses, direct or indirect, which are incurred because of the use of the information contained within this document, including, but not limited to, errors, omissions, or inaccuracies.

Under no circumstances will any blame or legal responsibility be held against the publisher, or author, for any damages, reparation, or monetary loss due to the information contained within this book. Either directly or indirectly. You are responsible for your own choices, actions, and results.

Published by:
Kent Jameson Publishing
16394 West Hilton Avenue
Goodyear, AZ 85338
kentjamesonpublishing@gmail.com
Printed in the United States of America.
First Printing, 2024
Library of Congress Cataloging-in-Publication Data:
Kent Jameson
The Grinning Gardener's Handbook Volume 1: A Comprehensive Guide To Growing amazing Fruits and Vegetables in Different Climates and Seasons

TABLE OF CONTENTS

Introduction — 7

1. FOUNDATIONS OF ORGANIC GARDENING — 11
   1.1 Understanding Organic Gardening — 12
   1.2 Soil Health and Composition — 14
   1.3 Building and Maintaining Compost — 15
   1.4 Organic Fertilizers and Amendments — 19

2. PLANNING YOUR GARDEN — 23
   2.1 Choosing the Right Location — 24
   2.2 Designing Your Garden Layout — 26
   2.3 Seasonal Planting Calendars — 29
   2.4 Companion Planting Strategies — 31

3. CLIMATE-SPECIFIC GARDENING — 35
   3.1 Gardening in Cold Climates — 36
   3.2 Hot and Arid Climate Gardening — 38
   3.3 Humid Climate Gardening — 40
   3.4 Coastal and Windy Climate Gardening — 42

4. GROWING VEGETABLES — 45
   4.1 Leafy Greens (Lettuce, Spinach, Kale) — 46
   4.2 Root Vegetables (Carrots, Beets, Radishes) — 48
   4.3 Nightshades (Tomatoes, Peppers, Eggplants) — 50
   4.4 Gourds and Squashes (Zucchini, Pumpkins, Cucumbers) — 53

5. GROWING EDIBLE FRUITS — 57
   5.1 Berry Bushes (Strawberries, Raspberries, Blueberries) — 58
   5.2 Melons (Watermelon, Cantaloupe, Honeydew) — 60
   5.3 Grapevines (Grapes, Kiwi) — 62
   5.4 Tropical Fruits for Temperate Climates (Pineapple, Passionfruit) — 64

6. SOIL AND WATER MANAGEMENT	67
6.1 Testing and Improving Soil pH	68
6.2 Efficient Watering Techniques	70
6.3 Drip Irrigation Systems	72
6.4 Mulching for Moisture Retention	74
7. PEST AND DISEASE CONTROL	79
7.1 Integrated Pest Management (IPM) Basics	80
7.2 Natural Pest Repellents	83
7.3 Beneficial Insects and Pollinators	85
7.4 Managing Common Plant Diseases	88
8. ADVANCED GARDENING TECHNIQUES	91
8.1 Grafting for Fruit Plants	92
8.2 Soil Blocking for Seed Starting	94
8.3 Vertical Gardening Solutions	96
8.4 Creating Microclimates in Your Garden	99
9. SUSTAINABLE AND ECO-FRIENDLY PRACTICES	103
9.1 Water Conservation Methods	104
9.2 Organic Weed Management	106
9.3 Crop Rotation and Soil Health	108
9.4 Building a Pollinator-Friendly Garden	110
10. HARVESTING AND STORAGE	113
10.1 Harvesting Techniques for Peak Ripeness	114
10.2 Storing Root Vegetables	116
10.3 Preserving Leafy Greens	117
10.4 Canning and Freezing Fruits	118
10.5 Preserving Leafy Greens	119
10.6 Canning and Freezing Fruits	121
11. TROUBLESHOOTING AND PROBLEM SOLVING	125
11.1 Diagnosing Nutrient Deficiencies	126
11.2 Dealing with Drought Stress	128
11.3 Addressing Overwatering Problems	130
11.4 Managing Poor Soil Drainage	132
12. INSPIRATIONAL CASE STUDIES AND RESOURCES	135
12.1 Success Stories from Home Gardeners	136
12.2 Community Gardening Projects	140

12.3 Online Resources and Gardening Communities	144
12.4 Continuing Education and Advanced Courses	146
Conclusion	149
References	153
Author Bio	159

INTRODUCTION

"The Grinning Gardener's Handbook Volume 1" was born out of a desire to share that joy and fulfillment with you. This book aims to be a comprehensive guide to growing amazing organic fruits and vegetables. Whether you're a seasoned gardener or just starting out, you'll find the knowledge and tools you need to cultivate a thriving organic garden.

Organic gardening is more than just a method; it's a philosophy that prioritizes sustainability and respect for the natural world. By choosing organic practices, you're not only producing healthier, more flavorful food but also contributing to a healthier environment. Organic gardening focuses on building rich, fertile soil through natural means, avoiding synthetic chemicals, and encouraging biodiversity. It's a holistic approach that seeks to create a balanced ecosystem where plants, insects, and soil microorganisms work together harmoniously.

In this handbook, you'll find detailed information on a wide range of topics that are crucial for successful organic gardening. We'll cover planting and growing techniques that are tailored to different climates and seasons. You'll learn about soil health management, fertilization methods, and effective weed control. We'll discuss watering strategies, drought tolerance, and natural insect control. Each chapter will provide specific growing information for different climates and seasons across the USA.

One of the most important aspects of this book is the tailored advice it offers for each type of edible fruit-bearing plant and vegetable. Every plant has unique needs, and understanding these needs is key to successful gardening. You'll find detailed guidance on planting depth, spacing, and the best seasons to plant and harvest each type of plant. Whether you're growing tomatoes in the heat of summer or kale in the cool of fall, you'll have the information you need to ensure healthy, productive plants.

My personal vision for this book is to empower you with the knowledge and confidence to grow your own organic garden. Gardening is a passion for me, and I've spent years studying and practicing sustainable techniques. Through this book, I hope to share my experiences and insights with you. I believe that anyone can cultivate a beautiful, productive garden with the right guidance and a bit of dedication.

The book is organized into several key chapters, each focusing on a different aspect of organic gardening. You'll start with the basics of soil preparation and move on to planting and caring for your garden. Each chapter includes practical tips, step-by-step guides, and troubleshooting sections to help you overcome common challenges. By the end of the book, you'll have a solid understanding of how to grow a wide variety of fruits and vegetables organically.

As you read through these pages, I encourage you to embrace the journey of gardening with an open heart and a curious mind. There's something incredibly rewarding about nurturing a plant from seed to harvest, knowing that your efforts are contributing to a healthier, more sustainable world. With the right knowledge and a bit of patience, you'll find that growing amazing organic fruits and vegetables is not only possible but deeply satisfying.

So, let's dig in together. Let's explore the wonders of organic gardening and discover the joy of cultivating your own green space. Whether you're growing a small container garden on your balcony or tending to a large backyard plot, this book will guide you every step of the way. The journey to a thriving organic garden starts here, and I couldn't be more excited to share it with you.

CHAPTER 1
FOUNDATIONS OF ORGANIC GARDENING

This chapter is dedicated to laying the groundwork for your organic garden, starting with a solid understanding of what organic gardening is and why it matters.

1.1 UNDERSTANDING ORGANIC GARDENING

Organic gardening is a method of growing plants that aligns with nature's processes. It avoids synthetic chemicals, emphasizes natural cycles, and promotes biodiversity. At its core, organic gardening is about creating a balanced ecosystem where plants, soil, and wildlife coexist harmoniously. This method relies on natural fertilizers like compost and manure, along with biological pest control methods, such as attracting beneficial insects. By avoiding synthetic chemicals, you reduce the risk of harmful residues in your food and minimize environmental pollution.

The principles of organic gardening focus on working with nature rather than against it. This means enhancing soil health through composting, crop rotation, and cover cropping. These practices build soil fertility and structure, making it more resilient and productive. Organic gardening also promotes biodiversity by encouraging a variety of plants and beneficial organisms. This diversity helps control pests and diseases naturally, reducing the need for chemical interventions. By following these principles, you create a garden that is sustainable and self-sufficient.

The benefits of organic gardening extend beyond your garden. For your health, organic produce is free from synthetic pesticides and fertilizers, making it safer to eat. Studies have shown that organic fruits and vegetables often contain higher levels of certain nutrients. Environmentally, organic gardening reduces pollution by avoiding chemical runoff that can contaminate water sources. It also enhances soil health, which is crucial for carbon sequestration and mitigating climate change. Promoting biodiversity supports local ecosystems, providing habitats for pollinators and other beneficial organisms.

Historically, organic gardening has deep roots in traditional farming practices. Before the advent of synthetic chemicals, farmers relied on natural methods to grow crops. Techniques like crop rotation, composting, and natural pest control were standard. However, the rise of industrial agriculture in the 20th century shifted the focus to chemical-intensive methods. This led to increased yields but also significant environmental damage. In response, the organic movement emerged, championed by pioneers like Sir Albert Howard and F.H. King. They advocated for a return to natural farming methods, laying the foundation for modern organic gardening practices. The publication of Rachel Carson's "Silent Spring" in the 1960s further fueled the movement, highlighting the dangers of pesticides and sparking widespread demand for organic food.

Despite its benefits, organic gardening is often misunderstood. One common misconception is that organic gardening is prohibitively expensive. While it's true that organic products can sometimes cost more, many organic gardening practices, like composting and mulching, are cost-effective. Another myth is that organic gardening is less productive than conventional methods. However, studies have shown that organic gardens can be just as productive, if not more so, over the long term. The focus on soil health and biodiversity creates a resilient system that can withstand pests and diseases better than chemically dependent gardens. Finally, some believe that organic gardening requires advanced technology or specialized knowledge. In reality, it relies on simple, time-tested practices that anyone can learn and implement.

Understanding organic gardening is the first step in creating a thriving, sustainable garden. By embracing these principles and practices, you contribute to a healthier environment and enjoy the benefits of fresh, nutritious produce. This chapter will guide you through the essentials, providing the knowledge you need to start your own organic garden.

1.2 SOIL HEALTH AND COMPOSITION

The heartbeat of any thriving garden lies beneath the surface, in the soil. Soil health is crucial for organic gardening because it directly influences the vitality and productivity of your plants. Think of soil as the foundation of plant health. Just as a strong building needs a solid foundation, your plants need healthy soil to flourish. Healthy soil teems with life, including bacteria, fungi, and earthworms, which all play a role in nutrient cycling. This process helps break down organic matter into nutrients that plants can absorb, ensuring they get the nourishment they need.

Now, let's break down the components that make up this essential foundation. Soil consists of minerals, organic matter, and living organisms. The mineral component includes sand, silt, and clay, each contributing to soil texture and drainage. Sand particles are large and create spaces that allow water to drain quickly, while clay particles are small and help retain moisture. Silt falls in between, providing a balance. Organic matter, or humus, is another critical component. It improves soil structure, increases water retention, and supplies nutrients. Then there are the living organisms, like earthworms and microbes, which enhance soil fertility by breaking down organic matter and releasing nutrients. Together, these components create a soil structure that supports plant roots, allowing them to access water, air, and nutrients efficiently.

Testing soil health is a key step in understanding your garden's needs. Start with a soil pH test to determine the acidity or alkalinity of your soil. Most plants prefer a pH between 6.0 and 7.0. You can use a home testing kit or send samples to a local extension service for more accurate results. Nutrient analysis is another important test. It will reveal levels of essential nutrients like nitrogen, phosphorus, and potassium. Additionally, a visual and tactile assessment can provide insights into soil texture and structure. For a simple test, take a handful of moist soil and squeeze it. If it forms a crumbly ball, you have good structure. If it's too loose or too sticky, adjustments may be needed.

Improving soil health naturally involves several practices. Adding organic matter, such as compost or leaf litter, is one of the best ways to boost soil fertility. Compost enriches the soil with nutrients and improves its structure. Mulching is another effective technique. Applying a layer of organic mulch, like straw or wood chips, helps retain moisture, suppress weeds, and add organic matter as it decomposes. Crop rotation and cover cropping are also invaluable. Rotating crops prevents nutrient depletion and reduces pests and disease buildup. Cover crops, like clover or rye, add organic matter and nutrients to the soil when tilled in.

Consider incorporating practical steps to maintain and enhance soil health. For example, after harvesting your summer vegetables, plant a cover crop in the fall. This will protect the soil from erosion and add organic matter when plowed under in the spring. Additionally, use a mix of green and brown materials in your compost to ensure a balanced nutrient profile. Regularly test your soil to monitor its health and adjust your practices accordingly. By focusing on soil health, you create a robust foundation for your plants, leading to a more productive and sustainable garden.

1.3 BUILDING AND MAINTAINING COMPOST

Composting is the heartbeat of organic gardening. It transforms everyday waste into nutrient-rich humus, a process that breathes life into your soil. At its core, compost is decomposed organic matter. This transformation occurs through the natural breakdown of kitchen scraps, yard waste, and other organic materials. The resulting compost improves soil structure, enhances fertility, and promotes healthy root development. By adding compost to your garden, you create a thriving environment for plants, allowing them to access essential nutrients naturally.

Composting involves a balance of green and brown materials. Green materials, rich in nitrogen, include vegetable scraps, coffee grounds, and grass clippings. These components provide the essential proteins and amino acids that microbes need to thrive. On the other hand, brown materials, high in carbon, include dried leaves, straw, and shredded paper. These elements add structure to the compost and help to aerate the pile. Avoid adding meat, dairy products, and diseased plants, as they can attract pests and slow down the decomposition process. A balanced mix of greens and browns ensures a healthy compost pile that breaks down efficiently.

There are several methods of composting, each suited to different garden setups and personal preferences.

Traditional compost bins

Traditional composting allows for easy layering of materials and regular turning. These bins can be made from wood, plastic, or metal and should be placed in a well-drained, sunny spot.

Vermicomposting

Vermicomposting uses worms to break down kitchen scraps into rich castings. This method is ideal for small spaces and can even be done indoors.

Bokashi composting

This compost style uses an anaerobic method that ferments food waste using a special bran. It's a compact, odorless option suitable for urban gardeners.

Trench composting

This style involves digging a trench in your garden, filling it with organic waste, and covering it with soil. This method is simple and requires minimal effort, making it a great choice for busy gardeners.

Maintaining compost requires regular attention to ensure it breaks down efficiently. Turning the compost regularly aerates the pile, promoting the activity of aerobic microbes that speed up decomposition. Aim to turn your compost every few weeks or whenever you add a significant amount of new material. Monitoring moisture levels is also crucial. The compost should be as damp as a wrung-out sponge. Too much moisture can lead to anaerobic conditions and foul odors, while too little can slow decomposition. Balancing green and brown materials helps maintain the right carbon-to-nitrogen ratio, ensuring a healthy microbial environment.

Checklist for Maintaining Compost

- Turn the compost every few weeks to aerate the pile.
- Monitor moisture levels, keeping the compost as damp as a wrung-out sponge.
- Balance green and brown materials to maintain the right carbon-to-nitrogen ratio.

- Add a mix of small, chopped materials to speed up decomposition.

When issues arise, troubleshooting common composting problems can keep your pile on track. If your compost smells unpleasant, it's likely too wet or contains too many greens. Add more brown materials and turn the pile to improve aeration. If the compost isn't breaking down, it may be too dry or need more nitrogen-rich greens. Add water and green materials, then mix thoroughly. Pests can be deterred by avoiding meat and dairy products and ensuring food scraps are buried within the pile. A well-maintained compost pile will break down efficiently, providing a steady supply of nutrient-rich humus for your garden.

A real-life example of composting's impact can be seen in community gardens. In urban areas, community gardens often face challenges with poor soil quality. By collectively composting kitchen scraps and yard waste, these gardens can produce rich humus that transforms the soil. Over time, the improved soil structure and fertility lead to healthier plants and more bountiful harvests, demonstrating the power of composting in even the most challenging environments.

By understanding and implementing these composting practices, you create a sustainable cycle of life in your garden. Each layer of vegetable scraps, each turn of the pile, and each handful of finished compost contributes to a thriving, vibrant garden. The effort you invest in composting pays dividends in the form of healthy soil and robust plants, making it a cornerstone of successful organic gardening.

1.4 ORGANIC FERTILIZERS AND AMENDMENTS

Understanding what organic fertilizers are and how they differ from synthetic ones is crucial for anyone committed to sustainable gardening. Organic fertilizers are derived from natural sources, such as plant residues, animal by-products, and minerals. Unlike synthetic fertilizers, which provide a quick nutrient boost but can harm soil health over time, organic fertilizers release nutrients slowly. This slow-release property ensures that plants receive a steady supply of nutrients, avoiding the peaks and troughs associated with synthetic options. The benefits of using organic fertilizers extend beyond immediate plant health. They improve soil structure, promote microbial activity, and help retain moisture, creating a robust environment for your plants to thrive.

There are several types of organic fertilizers, each with its unique advantages.

Animal-based fertilizers

This includes fertilizers such as manure and bone meal. These types are rich in nitrogen and phosphorus, essential for leafy growth and root development. Manure, whether from cows, chickens, or horses, adds organic matter to the soil, improving its texture and fertility. Bone meal, made from ground animal bones, is an excellent source of phosphorus and calcium, crucial for root growth and flowering.

Plant-based fertilizers

Fertilizers in this category include alfalfa meal and kelp which offer a balanced nutrient profile and improve soil structure. Alfalfa meal provides a slow-release source of nitrogen and trace minerals, while kelp adds potassium and a variety of micronutrients.

Mineral-based fertilizers

This category of fertilizers includes rock phosphate and greensand and supply essential minerals that may be lacking in your soil. Rock phosphate is an excellent source of phosphorus, while greensand provides potassium and trace minerals, improving soil fertility and structure over time.

Applying organic fertilizers effectively involves understanding the timing and methods best suited for your plants. The timing of application can vary depending on the specific needs of your garden. Generally, applying fertilizers before planting and during the growing season ensures that plants receive the nutrients they need when they need them most. Pre-planting applications help prepare the soil, giving seedlings a nutrient-rich environment to establish roots. During the growing season, side-dressing—placing fertilizer near the plant base—ensures that nutrients are readily available. Broadcasting, or evenly spreading fertilizer over a large area, is another method suitable for larger plots. Dosage and frequency are also critical; over-fertilizing can harm plants and the environment. Following recommended guidelines for each type of fertilizer ensures balanced nutrient availability without excess.

Soil amendments play a complementary role in organic gardening by improving soil structure and fertility. Adding lime, for instance, helps adjust the pH of acidic soils, making nutrients more accessible to plants. Lime is best applied in the fall, allowing it to react with the soil over the winter. Gypsum, another valuable amendment, improves soil structure by breaking up compacted clay soils and enhancing drainage. Incorporating organic matter, such as compost or well-rotted manure, boosts soil fertility and supports microbial activity. Organic matter improves soil structure, increasing its ability to retain water and nutrients.

Imagine preparing your garden beds for the upcoming season. Before planting, you test your soil and find it slightly acidic. To remedy this, you add lime, carefully working it into the soil. Next, you incorporate compost, enriching the soil with organic matter. As you plant your seedlings, you side-dress them with bone meal, ensuring they have the phosphorus needed for strong root development. Throughout the growing season, you monitor your plants and apply kelp as a foliar spray, providing additional nutrients and promoting robust growth. These practices, rooted in understanding and patience, transform your garden into a thriving, sustainable ecosystem.

Organic fertilizers and amendments are the building blocks of a healthy garden. They nourish plants, enrich the soil, and promote a balanced ecosystem. By understanding and applying these natural inputs, you create a foundation for long-term garden health and productivity. The knowledge and techniques shared here empower you to make informed choices, ensuring your garden thrives season after season. As you implement these practices, you'll see the profound impact of organic gardening on your plants and the environment.

CHAPTER 2
PLANNING YOUR GARDEN

This chapter will guide you through the essential steps of selecting the perfect location for your garden, ensuring your plants get the sunlight, soil quality, water, and protection they need.

2.1 CHOOSING THE RIGHT LOCATION

Choosing the right location for your garden is crucial for plant health and productivity. One of the first factors to consider is sunlight exposure. Sunlight is vital for photosynthesis, the process by which plants convert light into energy. Depending on your plants' needs, you'll need to assess different areas of your garden for sunlight levels. Full sun areas receive at least six hours of direct sunlight daily, ideal for sun-loving plants like tomatoes, peppers, and squash. Partial shade areas get about three to six hours of sunlight, suitable for plants like lettuce and spinach. Full shade areas receive less than three hours of direct sunlight, perfect for shade-tolerant plants like ferns and hostas.

To accurately evaluate sunlight levels, consider creating a sunlight map of your garden. Start by using a compass or a compass app on your phone to determine the direction your garden faces. South-facing gardens receive the most sun exposure, making them ideal for a wide variety of plants. North-facing gardens, on the other hand, receive the least sun, making them suitable for shade-tolerant plants. East-facing gardens get morning sunlight, which is gentler and perfect for plants sensitive to intense afternoon heat. West-facing gardens receive the strong afternoon sun, suitable for sun-loving plants that can handle heat.

Next, take photos of your garden every hour from 8:00 a.m. to 8:00 p.m. Note the areas that receive different levels of sunlight throughout the day. Label these areas as full sun, morning sun/afternoon shade, morning shade/afternoon sun, dappled shade, and full shade. This sunlight map will help you plan your garden layout, placing sun-loving plants in sunny spots, shade-loving plants in shady spots, and partial-sun plants in between. By understanding your garden's sunlight exposure, you can ensure each plant gets the light it needs to thrive.

Soil considerations are equally important when choosing your garden location. The type and quality of soil in different areas can significantly impact plant growth. Soil can be sandy, loamy, or clay, each with distinct characteristics. Sandy soil drains quickly but may lack nutrients. Loamy soil, a balanced mix of sand, silt, and clay, is ideal for most plants due to its good drainage and nutrient-holding capacity. Clay soil retains moisture well but can become compacted and drain poorly.

To identify your soil type, take a handful of moist soil and squeeze it. If it forms a loose ball that crumbles easily, it's sandy. If it forms a ball that holds its shape but feels gritty, it's loamy. If it forms a sticky ball that holds its shape and feels smooth, it's clay. Once you've identified your soil type, you can amend it to improve its quality. For sandy soil, add organic matter like compost to increase water and nutrient retention. For clay soil, incorporate coarse sand or gypsum to improve drainage and aeration. Regularly adding compost to any soil type enhances its fertility and structure, creating a healthier environment for your plants.

Water accessibility is another crucial factor. Ensure your garden location has adequate water access to keep your plants hydrated. Consider the proximity to water sources like outdoor faucets or rain barrels. If your garden is far from a water source, installing hose bibs or an irrigation system can make watering more convenient. Drip irrigation systems are particularly efficient, delivering water directly to the plant roots and reducing water waste. Grouping plants with similar water needs together also simplifies watering and ensures each plant gets the right amount of moisture.

Microclimates and wind protection are often overlooked but can significantly affect plant growth. A microclimate is a small area with different climatic conditions than its surroundings. These can be warmer, cooler, more humid, or drier than the general area. Identifying natural windbreaks like trees or buildings can help create microclimates that protect plants from harsh conditions. For example, a south-facing wall can create a warmer microclimate, ideal for heat-loving plants in cooler regions. Conversely, a shaded area under a tree can provide a cooler microclimate for shade-tolerant plants.

Wind protection is essential to prevent wind damage and reduce water loss. Natural barriers like trees and shrubs can act as windbreaks, reducing wind speed and creating a more stable environment for your plants. If natural windbreaks are not available, you can create artificial ones using hedges, fencing, or even strategically placed garden structures. For maximum protection, plant windbreaks at two to five times the mature height of the trees from the area you want to protect. Dense evergreen trees and shrubs are particularly effective, providing year-round wind protection and additional benefits like wildlife habitat and aesthetic appeal.

Choosing the right location for your garden involves careful consideration of sunlight, soil, water, and microclimates. By assessing these factors and making informed decisions, you create an environment where your plants can thrive. This thoughtful approach to planning will set the foundation for a successful and productive garden.

2.2 DESIGNING YOUR GARDEN LAYOUT

When it comes to designing your garden layout, choosing the right type of garden bed is crucial. Raised beds are a popular choice for many gardeners due to their numerous benefits. By elevating the soil, raised beds offer better control over soil quality and drainage. This is particularly advantageous if your native soil is poor or compacted. Raised beds also warm up more quickly in the spring, allowing for earlier planting. Constructing raised beds from materials like wood, stone, or recycled plastics provides a neat and organized look. They can be built to any height, making gardening more accessible and reducing the need for bending over, which is especially helpful for those with mobility issues.

In contrast, in-ground beds are ideal for larger garden spaces. They allow for expansive planting areas and are often easier to set up initially. In-ground beds rely on the existing soil, which means soil amendments and preparation are crucial. These beds are particularly suitable for crops that require a lot of space, such as pumpkins or corn. While they may not offer the same level of soil control as raised beds, in-ground beds can be highly productive with proper soil management.

Container gardening is another versatile option, especially for those with limited space. Containers can be placed on patios, balconies, or even windowsills, making gardening accessible in urban environments. They provide excellent control over soil conditions and can be moved to optimize sunlight exposure. Containers come in various sizes and materials, including plastic, clay, and fabric pots. Ensure that containers have adequate drainage holes to prevent waterlogging. This method is great for growing herbs, small vegetables, and even dwarf fruit trees, allowing you to enjoy fresh produce regardless of space constraints.

Designing pathways in your garden is essential for accessibility and ease of maintenance. Well-planned pathways ensure you can reach all parts of your garden without compacting the soil around your plants. A good rule of thumb is to make pathways at least 18 inches wide for comfortable movement. For wheelbarrow access, consider pathways that are 36 inches wide. Pathways can be made from various materials, each offering different benefits. Mulch pathways are soft underfoot and help suppress weeds. Gravel provides excellent drainage and a clean look. Pavers offer a solid surface that is easy to walk on and can be designed in various patterns for aesthetic appeal.

Crop rotation planning is a key strategy for maintaining soil health and managing pests. The principle of crop rotation involves changing the types of crops grown in each area of your garden each year. This practice helps prevent the buildup of pests and diseases specific to certain plant families. For instance, rotating crops by family groups, such as brassicas (cabbage, broccoli) and legumes (beans, peas), can break pest and disease cycles. Crop rotation also improves soil fertility by varying the nutrient demands of different plants. Legumes, for example, fix nitrogen in the soil, benefiting subsequent crops that require high nitrogen levels.

Creating a multi-year rotation plan involves mapping out your garden beds and assigning different crop families to each bed for each growing season. A common rotation cycle might include planting legumes in a bed one year, followed by brassicas the next, and then root vegetables like carrots and beets. This rotation ensures that no single nutrient is depleted from the soil and helps maintain a healthy balance. Planning crop rotations also spreads out the workload and reduces the need for chemical interventions, making your garden more sustainable.

Integrating perennials and annuals into your garden layout adds diversity and ensures continuous productivity. Designing perennial borders or sections in your garden provides a stable framework. Perennials, such as asparagus, rhubarb, and berry bushes, come back year after year, reducing the need for replanting and providing a reliable harvest. These plants often have deep root systems that improve soil structure and help retain moisture. Perennials can be used to create attractive and productive borders around garden beds or pathways.

On the other hand, planning annual beds for seasonal crops allows for flexibility and experimentation. Annuals, including tomatoes, peppers, and lettuce, complete their life cycle in one growing season, giving you the freedom to change your garden layout and try new varieties each year. Interplanting annuals and perennials can maximize space and enhance biodiversity. For example, you can plant annual herbs like basil and dill around perennial fruit trees to attract beneficial insects and improve pollination. This integration of perennials and annuals creates a dynamic and resilient garden ecosystem.

Designing your garden layout with these considerations in mind ensures a well-organized and productive space. By choosing the right garden bed types, planning accessible pathways, implementing crop rotation, and integrating perennials and annuals, you create a balanced and sustainable garden. This thoughtful approach to layout design not only enhances the health and productivity of your plants but also makes gardening a more enjoyable and rewarding experience.

2.3 SEASONAL PLANTING CALENDARS

Understanding planting seasons is fundamental to a successful garden. Different plants thrive in different temperatures and conditions and recognizing the distinction between cool-season and warm-season crops can make all the difference. Cool-season crops, such as lettuce, spinach, and peas, prefer the milder temperatures of spring and fall. These plants can tolerate light frosts and often bolt, or go to seed, in the heat of summer. On the other hand, warm season crops like tomatoes, peppers, and cucumbers flourish in the heat of summer and cannot survive frost. These crops need warm soil and consistent temperatures to grow and produce fruit. Transition periods between seasons are also crucial. The shift from spring to summer or summer to fall can be a window of opportunity for planting transitional crops that can bridge the gap and extend your harvest season.

Creating a personalized planting calendar is an invaluable tool. Start by determining the frost dates for your region, which are the average last frost date in spring and the first frost date in fall. These dates provide the framework for your planting schedule. You can find frost date information through local extension services or online gardening databases. Once you know your frost dates, you can schedule seed starting, transplanting, and direct sowing. Begin by listing your crops and noting whether they are cool-season or warm-season. For cool-season crops, plan to start seeds indoors about six to eight weeks before the last frost date. Warm-season crops can be started indoors four to six weeks before the last frost date and transplanted after the danger of frost has passed. Direct sowing, or planting seeds directly in the ground, can be done for crops like beans and carrots once the soil has warmed.

Succession planting is a technique that maximizes garden productivity by planning multiple harvests from the same space throughout the growing season. This method ensures a continuous supply of fresh produce and makes the most of limited garden space. For example, you can plant a fast-growing crop like lettuce in early spring. Once harvested, follow it with a summer crop like beans. After the beans are done, you can plant a fall crop like spinach. By carefully planning the timing and sequence of your plantings, you can keep your garden producing from early spring to late fall. Succession planting also helps reduce pest and disease pressure by not allowing any one crop to remain in the ground for too long.

Adjusting your planting calendar based on local climate variations is essential for adapting to unexpected weather changes. Using row covers or cold frames can protect young plants from late spring frosts or extend the growing season into the fall. Row covers are lightweight fabrics that can be draped over plants to provide a few degrees of frost protection. Cold frames are simple structures with transparent lids that trap heat and shelter plants from cold winds. These tools allow you to start planting earlier in the spring and continue harvesting later into the fall. In unusually hot or cold years, adjusting your planting times and choosing heat-tolerant or cold-tolerant varieties can help your garden thrive despite challenging conditions.

Understanding and planning for seasonal variations in your garden not only increases productivity but also enhances your gardening experience. By recognizing the needs of cool-season and warm-season crops, creating a detailed planting calendar, utilizing succession planting, and adapting to climate variations, you set the stage for a bountiful and resilient garden. This thoughtful approach ensures that you make the most of each growing season, providing a steady supply of fresh, organic produce for your table. As you refine your planning skills, you'll find that each season brings new opportunities and challenges, making gardening a rewarding and ever-evolving pursuit.

2.4 COMPANION PLANTING STRATEGIES

Companion planting is a time-honored practice that enhances plant health and boosts yields by leveraging the natural relationships between plants. This method involves strategically planting different species close together to benefit from their unique characteristics. One of the primary benefits of companion planting is natural pest control. Certain plant combinations can repel harmful insects, reducing the need for chemical pesticides. For example, planting marigolds around your garden can deter nematodes and aphids. Similarly, planting basil near tomatoes not only improves the flavor of the tomatoes but also repels mosquitoes and flies. This symbiotic relationship between plants creates a balanced ecosystem where pests are naturally managed, leading to healthier plants and better yields.

Improved pollination is another significant advantage of companion planting. Some plants attract beneficial insects that are crucial for pollinating fruits and vegetables. Flowers like borage and calendula, when planted near crops like cucumbers and squash, attract bees and other pollinators, ensuring better fruit set and increased productivity. Additionally, certain plants can provide physical support to their companions. For instance, corn can act as a natural trellis for climbing beans, while beans fix nitrogen in the soil, benefiting the corn. This mutual support not only maximizes space but also enhances the overall health of the garden.

Popular companion planting pairs demonstrate the practical application of these principles. Basil and tomatoes are a classic combination. Basil repels pests like aphids and whiteflies, which commonly attack tomatoes. Additionally, the aromatic oils in basil can enhance the flavor of tomatoes when grown nearby. Another effective pairing is carrots and onions. Carrots can repel onion flies, while onions deter carrot flies. This mutual protection reduces pest damage and results in healthier crops. Similarly, planting nasturtiums as a trap crop can attract aphids away from more valuable plants like roses or vegetables. Nasturtiums are particularly attractive to aphids, drawing them away and preventing infestations on other plants.

Trap crops and beneficial insects play a pivotal role in integrated pest management. Trap crops are sacrificial plants that lure pests away from main crops. For example, planting radishes as a trap crop can attract flea beetles, sparing your broccoli and cabbage. Dill and fennel, on the other hand, attract beneficial insects like ladybugs and parasitic wasps. These insects' prey on common garden pests such as aphids and caterpillars. By fostering a diverse plant community, you create a habitat that supports these beneficial insects, enhancing natural pest control and reducing the need for chemical interventions.

While companion planting offers numerous benefits, it's essential to avoid harmful plant combinations that can negatively affect each other. Some plants release chemicals through their roots or leaves that can inhibit the growth of neighboring plants. For instance, beans and onions should not be planted together. Onions release compounds that can stunt the growth of beans. Similarly, fennel should be kept away from most other plants. It releases allelopathic chemicals that can suppress the growth of nearby plants, making it a poor companion for many vegetables. By understanding these interactions, you can make informed decisions about plant placement, ensuring a harmonious and productive garden.

Incorporating companion planting strategies into your garden planning can lead to healthier plants, higher yields, and a more balanced ecosystem. This approach not only leverages the natural relationships between plants but also promotes biodiversity and sustainability. By carefully selecting plant combinations and fostering beneficial insects, you create a resilient garden that thrives without the need for synthetic chemicals. Whether you're growing vegetables, fruits, or ornamental plants, companion planting offers a holistic and effective way to enhance your garden's health and productivity.

As you plan your garden, consider the relationships between different plants and how they can support each other. By integrating companion planting strategies into your layout, you create a dynamic and thriving garden that benefits from the natural interactions between plants. This thoughtful approach to planting not only maximizes your garden's potential but also contributes to a more sustainable and environmentally friendly gardening practice.

In the next chapter, we will explore the specifics of growing a variety of vegetables, focusing on techniques and tips that will help you cultivate a bountiful harvest.

CHAPTER 3
CLIMATE-SPECIFIC GARDENING

Gardening in cold climates presents unique challenges but also offers the joy of nurturing life in an environment that many would consider inhospitable. This chapter is dedicated to helping you understand how to thrive in these conditions, ensuring a bountiful harvest despite the chill.

3.1 GARDENING IN COLD CLIMATES

Selecting cold-hardy plants is the first step towards a successful garden in cooler regions. Cold-tolerant vegetables like kale, spinach, and carrots are your best allies. Kale is renowned for its ability to withstand frost, and its flavor even improves after a cold snap. Spinach, another hardy green, can be planted from mid-August to early October, giving you a chance to harvest through the winter. Carrots are also remarkably resilient; their roots develop a sweeter flavor as temperatures drop. For fruit-bearing plants, consider raspberries and gooseberries. Raspberries are particularly robust, providing a generous yield even in cooler climates. Gooseberries, with their tart yet sweet fruit, are also well-suited to withstand the cold. Both can be a delightful addition to your garden, offering fresh, homegrown fruit even in less-than-ideal weather.

Extending the growing season is crucial in cold climates, where the window for cultivation can be quite short. Using cold frames and cloches is a practical method to protect plants from early frosts and extend the growing season into the colder months. Cold frames are simple structures with transparent lids that trap heat, creating a microclimate that can be several degrees warmer than the surrounding air. Cloches, which are individual covers placed over plants, offer similar protection. Installing high tunnels or hoop houses can also provide a significant advantage. These structures, typically made of plastic stretched over a frame, create a greenhouse-like environment that allows you to start plants earlier in the spring and continue growing later into the fall. Utilizing row covers, lightweight fabrics that shield plants from frost and wind, can also make a substantial difference. They can be draped directly over plants or supported by hoops, providing a few degrees of frost protection and helping to retain warmth.

Preparing and maintaining soil for cold weather gardening is another essential aspect. Adding organic matter to your soil can improve its insulation properties, helping to retain warmth and moisture. Compost, well-rotted manure, and leaf mold are excellent choices. These materials not only enhance soil structure but also provide a slow-release source of nutrients that support plant growth throughout the colder months. Mulching is another effective technique. A thick layer of mulch, such as straw, wood chips, or shredded leaves, can act as a blanket, insulating the soil and maintaining a more stable temperature. Mulch also helps retain soil moisture, reducing the need for frequent watering and protecting plant roots from freezing.

Frost protection methods are vital for safeguarding your plants against unexpected cold snaps. Covering plants with frost blankets is a straightforward and effective approach. These blankets, made of lightweight, breathable fabric, can be draped over plants to provide a few degrees of protection. For added warmth, consider using water-filled plastic jugs as thermal mass. During the day, these jugs absorb heat from the sun, and at night, they release it, helping to keep the surrounding area warmer. Timing your plantings to avoid frost-sensitive stages is also crucial. For example, planting cold-tolerant crops like spinach and kale earlier in the season allows them to establish before the first frost, while more sensitive plants like tomatoes and peppers should be planted after the danger of frost has passed.

By understanding and implementing these strategies, you can overcome the challenges of gardening in cold climates. Selecting the right plants, extending the growing season, preparing your soil, and protecting against frost are all steps that will help you create a thriving, productive garden, even in the face of chilly temperatures.

3.2 HOT AND ARID CLIMATE GARDENING

Gardening in hot and arid climates can be quite challenging, but with the right strategies and plant choices, you can create a thriving garden. Drought-tolerant plants are your best allies in these conditions. Fruits and vegetables like okra, eggplant, and certain tomato breeds have evolved to withstand periods of low water availability. Okra, with its deep roots, can tap into moisture far below the surface, making it an excellent choice for dry regions. Eggplant, another heat lover, produces glossy fruits even under intense sun. Certain tomato varieties, such as 'Roma' and 'San Marzano,' are particularly drought-resistant and can provide a bountiful harvest with minimal water. Additionally, incorporating xerophytic plants like succulents as companion plants can further enhance your garden's resilience. These plants store water in their leaves, helping to create a microclimate that reduces evaporation and conserves moisture for neighboring plants.

Efficient watering techniques are crucial for conserving water and ensuring your plants get the moisture they need. Drip irrigation systems are highly effective in arid climates. These systems deliver water directly to the plant roots, minimizing evaporation and reducing water waste. You can set up a drip irrigation system using a network of tubes and emitters that can be customized to your garden layout. Another strategy is mulching. Applying a thick layer of mulch, such as straw, wood chips, or compost, helps to reduce evaporation by shading the soil and keeping it cool. Mulch also improves soil structure and adds organic matter as it decomposes, further enhancing moisture retention. Watering your garden early in the morning or late in the evening can also make a significant difference. During these times, temperatures are cooler, and evaporation rates are lower, allowing your plants to absorb more water before the heat of the day sets in.

Protecting your plants from intense sun and drying winds is essential for their survival in hot climates. Installing shade cloths or shade tunnels can provide much-needed relief from the scorching sun. Shade cloths are available in various densities, allowing you to control the amount of sunlight your plants receive. These cloths can be draped over a simple frame or attached to existing structures to create shaded areas in your garden. Shade tunnels, which are similar to high tunnels but covered with shade cloth instead of plastic, offer a more enclosed environment that protects plants from both sun and wind. Windbreaks, such as hedges or fences, can also play a vital role in protecting your garden. Fast-growing trees and shrubs, planted strategically around your garden, can reduce wind speed and create a more stable microclimate. Fences or trellises can provide additional wind protection, helping to reduce moisture loss and prevent wind damage to delicate plants.

Managing soil in arid regions involves techniques to retain moisture and nutrients. Incorporating organic matter into your soil is one of the most effective ways to improve its water-holding capacity. Compost, well-rotted manure, and leaf mold are excellent additions that enhance soil structure and fertility. These materials help create a network of organic particles that retain water and nutrients, making them more available to plant roots. Another useful amendment is hydrogels or water-absorbing crystals. These synthetic polymers can absorb many times their weight in water and release it slowly over time, providing a steady supply of moisture to your plants. Mixing hydrogels into your soil can significantly extend the time between waterings, making them particularly valuable in arid climates. Utilizing no-till gardening methods can also help preserve soil moisture. By avoiding tilling, you maintain the soil structure and protect the organic matter on the surface. This layer acts as a barrier, reducing evaporation and preserving moisture in the root zone. No-till methods also promote the health of soil microorganisms, which play a crucial role in nutrient cycling and soil fertility.

By selecting drought-tolerant plants, implementing efficient watering techniques, protecting your plants from sun and wind, and managing your soil effectively, you can create a productive garden even in the most challenging hot and arid climates.

3.3 HUMID CLIMATE GARDENING

Gardening in humid climates requires a bit of finesse, but with the right strategies, you can create a lush and productive garden. One of the first steps is selecting disease-resistant varieties that can withstand the challenges posed by high humidity. Mildew-resistant cucumbers and squash are excellent choices. These plants have been bred to resist the powdery and downy mildews that thrive in moist conditions. Similarly, tomatoes resistant to blight and fungal infections can save you a lot of headaches. Varieties like 'Celebrity' and 'Big Beef' are known for their resistance to common diseases like early blight and fusarium wilt. By choosing these resilient varieties, you reduce the risk of disease and increase your chances of a successful harvest.

Managing excess moisture is crucial in humid climates where heavy rains can lead to waterlogged soil. Raised beds are a practical solution to improve drainage. By elevating the soil, raised beds allow excess water to drain away more easily, preventing root rot and other moisture-related issues. Incorporating sand or perlite into your soil mix can further enhance drainage. These materials create air pockets in the soil, allowing water to flow through more freely. Installing French drains or swales around your garden can also help manage excess water. French drains are trenches filled with gravel and a perforated pipe that redirects water away from your garden beds. Swales, shallow channels designed to capture and redirect runoff, can prevent water from pooling in low areas. These techniques ensure your plants have the well-drained soil they need to thrive.

Pest control in humid climates often requires a proactive approach, as warm, moist conditions are ideal for many pests. Encouraging beneficial insects like predatory beetles and parasitic wasps can be an effective way to keep pest populations in check. These insects naturally prey on common garden pests, reducing the need for chemical interventions. Planting flowers like marigolds, dill, and fennel can attract these beneficial insects to your garden. Additionally, using neem oil or insecticidal soaps can help manage pests without harming the environment. Neem oil, derived from the neem tree, disrupts the life cycle of many pests, while insecticidal soaps work by breaking down the outer shell of soft-bodied insects like aphids and spider mites. Regularly inspecting your plants and applying these treatments as needed can keep pest problems under control.

Air circulation and plant spacing are vital for preventing fungal diseases in humid environments. Proper spacing of plants ensures good airflow, reducing the humidity around the foliage and making it harder for fungal spores to thrive. For instance, when planting tomatoes, leave at least two feet between each plant to allow air to circulate freely. Pruning plants to remove excess foliage can also improve air movement. For example, thinning out the lower leaves of tomato plants can help prevent diseases like early blight. The use of fans or natural wind corridors can further enhance air circulation. Placing a small fan in a greenhouse or using the natural layout of your garden to channel wind can make a significant difference. By keeping the air moving, you reduce the chances of fungal diseases taking hold.

By selecting the right plant varieties, managing soil moisture, implementing effective pest control strategies, and ensuring good air circulation, you can create a thriving garden in even the most humid climates. These techniques will help you overcome the challenges posed by high humidity, ensuring your plants remain healthy and productive.

3.4 COASTAL AND WINDY CLIMATE GARDENING

Gardening in coastal and windy climates brings its own set of challenges, but with the right strategies, you can cultivate a thriving garden. One of the first considerations is selecting salt-tolerant plants. Coastal environments often have high soil salinity, which can be tough on many plants. However, some fruits and vegetables thrive in these conditions. Asparagus, for instance, not only tolerates salty soil but also benefits from it, resulting in more robust spears. Beets and kale also perform well in coastal conditions, with kale's hardy leaves standing up to both salt and wind. Coastal herbs like rosemary and thyme are equally resilient, offering aromatic flavors that can enhance any dish. These plants have adapted to withstand salty air and soil, making them ideal choices for your coastal garden.

Protecting your plants from strong coastal winds is essential for their survival and growth. Windbreaks are a highly effective method for reducing wind speed and shielding your garden. Fast-growing trees and shrubs, such as willows or poplars, can be planted around the perimeter of your garden to act as natural barriers. These windbreaks not only protect your plants but also create a microclimate that can be several degrees warmer than the surrounding area. Another technique is using flexible plant supports and staking. For taller plants like tomatoes or beans, sturdy stakes and flexible ties can prevent wind damage. These supports allow the plants to sway slightly in the wind, reducing the risk of breaking. Wind-resistant gardening techniques help create a stable environment where your plants can thrive despite the gusts.

Managing soil salinity is crucial for maintaining healthy plants in coastal areas. One effective method is leaching, which involves flushing the soil with plenty of freshwater to wash away excess salts. This technique requires a consistent and generous supply of water, so it's best done during the rainy season or when water is readily available. Adding organic matter to your soil can also improve its structure and reduce salinity. Compost, well-rotted manure, and leaf mold increase the soil's ability to retain moisture and nutrients, diluting the concentration of salt. These organic materials create a more hospitable environment for plant roots, allowing them to access the water and nutrients they need.

Coastal areas often experience unique humidity and temperature fluctuations, which can be challenging for gardeners. Using mulch is an effective strategy to moderate soil temperature and retain moisture. A thick layer of mulch, such as straw, wood chips, or shredded leaves, acts as an insulating blanket, protecting the soil from extreme temperature changes. Mulch also helps to conserve soil moisture, reducing the need for frequent watering. Choosing plants that can tolerate a wide range of temperatures is another key to success. Varieties that are both heat-tolerant and cold-hardy will be more resilient to the unpredictable weather patterns of coastal regions. Installing shade structures can provide additional protection from sudden heat waves. Simple structures like shade cloths or pergolas can shield your plants from intense sun, preventing heat stress and sunburn. These structures can be adjusted or removed as needed, offering flexibility in adapting to changing conditions.

As you navigate the complexities of coastal and windy climate gardening, remember that the right plant choices and protective measures can make all the difference. By selecting salt-tolerant varieties, implementing wind-resistant techniques, managing soil salinity, and addressing humidity and temperature fluctuations, you can create a resilient and productive garden. Each of these strategies contributes to a balanced ecosystem where your plants can flourish despite the challenges of a coastal environment.

By understanding and implementing these climate-specific strategies, you are well on your way to creating a garden that thrives regardless of your local conditions. From cold to hot, humid to coastal, each environment presents unique challenges and opportunities. Embracing these differences allows you to grow a diverse and robust garden, tailored to your specific climate. In the next chapter, we will delve into the intricacies of growing vegetables, focusing on techniques and tips that will help you cultivate a bountiful harvest.

CHAPTER 4
GROWING VEGETABLES

I n this chapter, we will explore the optimal growing conditions, planting techniques, maintenance, and pest management for leafy greens like lettuce, spinach, and kale.

4.1 LEAFY GREENS (LETTUCE, SPINACH, KALE)

Leafy greens flourish in cool temperatures and partial shade. These conditions mimic their natural habitats and help them grow tender, flavorful leaves. Ideally, the temperature should range between 55°F and 70°F (NDSU Agriculture). Planting in a spot that receives morning sun and afternoon shade can protect your greens from the intense midday heat, which can cause them to bolt, or go to seed prematurely. Well-draining, fertile soil rich in organic matter is also crucial. This type of soil retains moisture without becoming waterlogged, providing a stable environment for your plants. Adding compost or well-rotted manure can boost soil fertility, ensuring your greens have the nutrients they need.

When it comes to planting, you have two main options: direct sowing and transplanting seedlings.

Direct Sowing

This planting style involves sowing seeds directly into the garden bed. This method is straightforward and works well for most leafy greens. Sow seeds in rows or blocks, spacing them according to the type of green. For instance, space lettuce seeds about 12 inches apart, while spinach can be spaced 6 inches apart.

Transplanting Seedlings

This planting style involves starting seeds indoors and moving the young plants to the garden once they are sturdy enough. This approach can give you a head start on the growing season. When transplanting, handle seedlings gently and space them as you would for direct sowing. Ensure they are planted at the same depth they were in their pots to avoid stress.

Maintaining and caring for leafy greens throughout the growing season involves a few key practices. Regular watering is essential to keep the soil consistently moist. Aim to provide about 1 to 1.5 inches of water per week, adjusting based on weather conditions. Mulching around your plants can help retain moisture and suppress weeds, reducing the need for frequent watering and weeding. Use organic mulches like straw, wood chips, or shredded leaves, which also add nutrients to the soil as they decompose. Thinning seedlings is another important step. Crowded plants compete for light, water, and nutrients, leading to poor growth. Thin your seedlings to the recommended spacing once they have a few true leaves. This practice improves air circulation, reducing the risk of disease.

Pest and disease management is crucial for healthy leafy greens. Aphids are a common pest that can damage young leaves and spread diseases. To control aphids, use neem oil or insecticidal soap, applying it in the early morning or late evening to avoid harming beneficial insects. Slugs and snails are also attracted to the tender leaves of leafy greens. Hand-pick these pests in the early morning or set up beer traps to lure and drown them. Downy mildew is a fungal disease that thrives in humid conditions and can cause yellowing and wilting of leaves. To prevent downy mildew, ensure proper plant spacing and good air circulation. Avoid overhead watering, which can create a moist environment conducive to fungal growth.

Instead, water at the base of the plants to keep the foliage dry. If you notice signs of mildew, remove affected leaves promptly and dispose of them away from the garden to prevent the spread of spores.

Leafy Greens Care Checklist

- Ensure cool temperatures and partial shade.
- Plant in well-draining, fertile soil with high organic matter.
- Water regularly to keep the soil consistently moist.
- Use organic mulch to retain moisture and suppress weeds.
- Thin seedlings to improve air circulation.
- Control aphids with neem oil or insecticidal soap.
- Hand-pick slugs and snails or use beer traps.
- Prevent downy mildew with proper spacing and base watering.

By understanding these optimal growing conditions and implementing effective planting and care techniques, you can enjoy a bountiful harvest of leafy greens. These practices not only enhance the health and productivity of your plants but also contribute to a sustainable and rewarding gardening experience.

4.2 ROOT VEGETABLES (CARROTS, BEETS, RADISHES)

Root vegetables, such as carrots, beets, and radishes, require particular attention to soil preparation. The key to growing healthy root vegetables lies in having deep, loose, and well-draining soil. This type of soil allows the roots to grow straight and reach their full potential. Compacted or heavy clay soils can lead to deformed or stunted roots. Therefore, it's crucial to loosen the soil to a depth of at least 12 inches. Removing rocks, debris, and clods is equally important. These obstacles can impede root growth and cause the vegetables to become misshapen. Adding compost to the soil not only improves its fertility but also enhances its structure, making it easier for roots to penetrate. Compost adds essential nutrients that support the growth of robust, healthy plants.

When it comes to planting root vegetables, direct seeding is the most effective method. This involves sowing seeds directly into the garden bed. Timing is crucial for direct seeding. For cool-season vegetables like carrots and radishes, it's best to sow seeds in early spring or late summer. Beets can be planted in both spring and fall. The ideal planting depth varies by vegetable: carrots should be sown about 1/4 inch deep, beets 1/2 inch deep, and radishes 1/2 inch deep. Proper spacing is also vital to ensure healthy growth. Carrots should be spaced about 2 inches apart, beets 3 to 4 inches apart, and radishes 1 inch apart. This spacing allows each plant enough room to develop without competing for nutrients, water, and sunlight.

Thinning and maintenance are critical steps in growing root vegetables. Once seedlings emerge, thinning them is necessary to avoid overcrowding. Thin carrot seedlings to 2 inches apart, beet seedlings to 4 inches apart, and radish seedlings to 1 inch apart. This practice ensures that each plant has sufficient space to grow. Regular weeding is also essential. Weeds compete with root vegetables for nutrients and water, so keeping the garden bed weed-free helps your vegetables thrive. Watering practices should focus on maintaining consistent soil moisture. Root vegetables require even moisture to develop properly. Water deeply and regularly, especially during dry periods, to keep the soil moist but not waterlogged.

Harvesting root vegetables at the right time is crucial for the best flavor and texture. Carrots are ready to harvest when they reach a diameter of about 3/4 inch. Beets are typically harvested when they are 1.5 to 3 inches in diameter, while radishes are best picked when they are about 1 inch in diameter. To harvest, gently loosen the soil around the roots with a garden fork or trowel, then pull the vegetables by their tops. Be careful not to damage the roots in the process. Proper storage is essential to keep your root vegetables fresh. Store them in cool, dark, and humid conditions. A root cellar or a refrigerator crisper drawer works well. For long-term storage, pack the vegetables in damp sand or sawdust to maintain humidity and prevent them from drying out.

Root vegetables are a rewarding addition to any garden, providing delicious and nutritious produce. By focusing on soil preparation, planting guidelines, thinning, maintenance, and proper harvesting and storage techniques, you can enjoy a bountiful harvest of carrots, beets, and radishes. These practices not only enhance the health and productivity of your plants but also contribute to a sustainable and fulfilling gardening experience.

4.3 NIGHTSHADES (TOMATOES, PEPPERS, EGGPLANTS)

Starting nightshade seeds indoors is a rewarding process that sets the stage for a fruitful garden. Begin by using seed starting trays filled with a sterile potting mix. This mix is essential as it provides a disease-free environment for your seedlings to thrive. Place the trays in a warm, sunny spot or under grow lights, maintaining an optimal temperature of 70°F to 80°F for germination. Light is crucial, so if using grow lights, keep them on for about 14 to 16 hours a day. Timing is everything; start your seeds six to eight weeks before the last expected frost date in your area. This gives your seedlings ample time to develop strong roots and sturdy stems before transplanting them outdoors.

Once your seedlings have grown to a healthy size, it's time to prepare them for the transition to the garden. Hardening off is a vital step that involves gradually exposing your seedlings to outdoor conditions. Start by placing them outside in a sheltered spot for a few hours each day, increasing the time and exposure to direct sunlight over a week or two. This process helps them acclimate to the outdoor environment, reducing the risk of transplant shock. When transplanting, space tomatoes about 24 to 36 inches apart, peppers 18 to 24 inches, and eggplants 24 to 30 inches. Plant them at the same depth they were in their pots, or for tomatoes, a bit deeper to encourage additional root growth. Support structures like cages or stakes are essential for tomatoes and peppers. These supports help keep the plants upright, preventing the fruit from touching the ground and reducing the risk of disease.

Caring for nightshade plants involves regular watering and mulching to retain soil moisture. Water deeply and consistently, aiming to keep the soil evenly moist but not waterlogged. Mulching around the base of the plants helps retain moisture, suppress weeds, and maintain an even soil temperature. Pruning is another important care practice, especially for tomatoes. Remove the lower leaves and any suckers that form between the main stem and branches. This promotes better air circulation and directs the plant's energy towards fruit production. For peppers and eggplants, pruning is less intensive but still beneficial. Remove any damaged or diseased leaves and thin out excess foliage to improve airflow.

Fertilization is key to healthy nightshade plants. Use organic fertilizers, such as compost or well-rotted manure, to provide a steady supply of nutrients. Start with a balanced fertilizer at planting time, then switch to a high-phosphorus fertilizer as the plants begin to flower and set fruit. This encourages robust root development and abundant fruiting. Regular feeding every few weeks throughout the growing season ensures your plants have the nutrients they need to thrive.

Managing pests and diseases is crucial for nightshades. Tomato hornworms are a common pest that can decimate your plants. Handpicking is an effective control method, as these large, green caterpillars are easy to spot. Alternatively, use Bacillus thuringiensis (Bt), a natural bacterial insecticide, to target hornworms without harming beneficial insects. Blossom end rot, a disorder affecting tomatoes, peppers, and eggplants, is caused by a calcium deficiency and inconsistent watering. To prevent it, maintain even soil moisture and add calcium supplements if needed. Removing affected fruits can help the plant focus on producing healthy new growth. Regularly inspect your plants for signs of disease, such as yellowing leaves or dark spots, and act promptly to prevent the spread.

By mastering these techniques, you can cultivate healthy, productive nightshade plants that yield abundant harvests. From the initial seed starting to transplanting and ongoing care, each step plays a crucial role in the success of your garden.

4.4 GOURDS AND SQUASHES (ZUCCHINI, PUMPKINS, CUCUMBERS)

Gourds and squashes, including zucchini, pumpkins, and cucumbers, thrive with the right planting techniques. Direct sowing is often the best method for these plants, particularly in warmer climates where the soil temperature is consistently above 60°F. This approach allows seeds to germinate and establish quickly in their final growing spot, reducing transplant shock. For those in cooler regions, starting seeds indoors can give your plants a head start. Use biodegradable pots to minimize root disturbance when transplanting. Prepare your garden bed by mounding the soil into small hills, about 12 inches high and 18 inches wide. This technique improves drainage and warms the soil faster, providing an ideal environment for germination. Space your mounds about 3 to 4 feet apart for zucchini and smaller squashes, and up to 6 feet apart for larger pumpkins to accommodate their sprawling growth habits.

Training and supporting gourd and squash plants can help manage their vigorous growth and improve air circulation. Cucumbers, in particular, benefit from vertical growth. Using trellises not only saves space but also keeps the fruit cleaner and reduces disease risk. You can create a simple trellis with wooden stakes and garden twine or opt for more elaborate structures like arches or A-frames. Smaller squashes and gourds can also be trained to climb, reducing their footprint and making harvesting easier. Pruning and training vines is essential to manage space and improve airflow. Regularly pinch off the growing tips of the vines to encourage bushier growth and remove any diseased or damaged leaves to prevent the spread of infections. Proper spacing and pruning reduces the risk of fungal diseases and ensure that sunlight reaches all parts of the plant.

Pollination is crucial for fruit set in gourds and squashes, and these plants rely heavily on pollinators like bees. Encourage pollinators by planting companion flowers such as marigolds, sunflowers, and borage around your garden. These flowers attract bees and other beneficial insects, improving pollination rates. In cases where natural pollination is insufficient, hand-pollination can be a valuable technique. Use a small paintbrush or cotton swab to transfer pollen from the male flowers (which have thin stems) to the female flowers (which have a small swelling at the base, indicating the developing fruit). This method ensures that each flower receives enough pollen to produce a healthy fruit.

Harvesting gourds and squashes at the right time is key to enjoying their best flavor and texture. For zucchini, harvest when the fruits are 6 to 8 inches long for the best taste. Pumpkins and winter squashes should be harvested when their skins are hard and cannot be easily pierced with a fingernail. This usually occurs in late summer or early fall. Use a sharp knife or pruning shears to cut the fruit from the vine, leaving a few inches of stem attached to prevent rot. Handle the fruits gently to avoid bruising, which can lead to spoilage. Proper storage is essential to extend the shelf life of your harvest. Store gourds and squashes in a cool, dry place with good air circulation. Avoid stacking them, as this can cause bruising and promote mold growth. Pumpkins and winter squashes can be stored for several months if kept at temperatures between 50°F and 55°F with low humidity. Check stored fruits regularly and remove any that show signs of decay to prevent it from spreading to others.

By mastering these techniques, you can cultivate a garden full of healthy, productive gourd and squash plants. From planting to harvesting, each step is an opportunity to nurture and enjoy the fruits of your labor. As you implement these practices, you'll find that these robust plants not only provide a bountiful harvest but also add a vibrant, dynamic element to your garden.

In this chapter, we've delved into the intricacies of growing a variety of vegetables, from leafy greens to nightshades and gourds. Each type of vegetable requires specific techniques and care to thrive, and understanding these needs sets the foundation for a successful garden. Next, we'll explore the world of edible fruits, offering detailed guidance to help you cultivate a productive and diverse garden year-round.

CHAPTER 5
GROWING EDIBLE FRUITS

G rowing your own berry bushes can transform even a small garden into a haven of delicious, organic produce. In this chapter, we'll dive into the specifics of cultivating these delightful fruits, ensuring you have all the knowledge needed to nurture them to their full potential.

5.1 BERRY BUSHES (STRAWBERRIES, RASPBERRIES, BLUEBERRIES)

Berry bushes thrive under specific conditions that mimic their natural habitats. Full sun exposure is crucial, as it helps berries develop their sweetness and ensures robust growth. Aim for at least six to eight hours of direct sunlight daily. In addition to sunlight, well-draining, slightly acidic soil is key. A pH range of 5.5 to 6.5 is ideal for most berry bushes. This acidity helps the plants absorb essential nutrients. To achieve this, you might need to amend your soil with organic matter like compost or pine needles, which naturally lower the pH. Adequate spacing is also important to promote air circulation and reduce the risk of fungal diseases. For strawberries, space plants about 18 inches apart. Raspberries require more room, with rows spaced 4 to 6 feet apart and plants spaced 2 to 3 feet apart within rows. Blueberries need even more space, with plants spaced about 4 to 5 feet apart.

Planting berry bushes involves some specific techniques to ensure they establish well. For strawberries, dig a hole deep enough to cover the roots without burying the crown, which should sit just above the soil surface. Raspberries benefit from being planted slightly deeper than they were in the nursery, with the root ball covered by about 1 to 2 inches of soil. Blueberries should be planted at the same depth as they were in their pots. Timing is also crucial. Bare-root plants are best planted in early spring before new growth starts, while potted plants can be planted in spring or fall. Ensure the planting hole is wide enough to spread the roots without bending them, and water thoroughly after planting to settle the soil around the roots.

Maintaining berry bushes throughout the growing season requires regular care and attention. Keeping the soil consistently moist is vital, as berry bushes have shallow roots that can dry out quickly. Water deeply once or twice a week, depending on rainfall and temperature, aiming to keep the soil evenly moist but not waterlogged. Mulching around the base of the plants with straw, wood chips, or pine needles helps retain moisture, suppress weeds, and maintain a stable soil temperature. Pruning is another essential task. For strawberries, remove runners to direct the plant's energy towards fruit production. Raspberries benefit from annual pruning to remove old canes and encourage new growth. After the fruiting season, cut back the old canes to the ground, leaving the new canes to produce next year's crop. Blueberries require less pruning but still benefit from the removal of dead or diseased wood and the thinning of older branches to promote air circulation.

Pest and disease management is crucial to protect your berry bushes and ensure a healthy harvest. Aphids are a common pest that can be controlled with insecticidal soap. Apply the soap in the early morning or late evening to avoid harming beneficial insects. Fungal diseases like powdery mildew thrive in humid conditions and can be managed by ensuring proper spacing and good air circulation. Avoid overhead watering, which can create a moist environment conducive to fungal growth. Instead, water at the base of the plants. Using netting to protect your berries from birds is also important. Birds love ripe berries as much as we do, and without protection, they can quickly decimate your crop. Drape bird netting over your bushes, securing it to the ground to prevent birds from getting underneath.

By understanding and implementing these practices, you can cultivate a thriving berry patch that provides delicious, organic fruit year after year. Whether you're growing strawberries, raspberries, or blueberries, the joy of harvesting fresh berries from your own garden is a gratifying reward.

5.2 MELONS (WATERMELON, CANTALOUPE, HONEYDEW)

Growing melons like watermelon, cantaloupe, and honeydew begins with proper soil preparation. These fruits thrive in well-draining, fertile soil enriched with high organic matter. If your soil is heavy clay or sandy, amend it by adding compost or aged manure. This not only improves soil structure but also enhances its fertility, providing essential nutrients for healthy plant growth. Ensuring the soil pH falls between 6.0 and 6.8 is crucial. Slightly acidic conditions help melons absorb nutrients more efficiently. You can test your soil pH using a home test kit or by sending a sample to a local extension service. If the pH is too high, sulfur can be added to lower it. Conversely, if the pH is too low, lime can help raise it to the desired level.

When it comes to planting melons, you have two main options: direct sowing or starting seeds indoors. Direct sowing is ideal if you live in a region where the soil temperature has consistently reached at least 70°F. This method allows seeds to germinate directly in the garden, minimizing transplant shock. For those in cooler climates, starting seeds indoors can give your plants a head start. Use peat pots or biodegradable containers to make transplanting easier. Plant melon seeds about half an inch deep in well-prepared soil. Creating mounds or hills for planting is a beneficial technique. These mounds improve drainage and help warm the soil, which is vital for seed germination and root development.

Space mounds about 3 to 4 feet apart for watermelons and 2 to 3 feet apart for cantaloupe and honeydew to accommodate their sprawling growth. Training and supporting melon plants can maximize your garden space and improve fruit quality. Using trellises for vertical growth is particularly effective for smaller melons like cantaloupe and honeydew. This method not only saves space but also keeps the fruits off the ground, reducing the risk of rot and pest damage. For larger melons like watermelons, which can be too heavy for trellises, consider pruning techniques to encourage larger fruit development. Remove any small or misshapen fruits to allow the plant to focus its energy on producing a few high-quality melons. Supporting heavy fruits with slings or netting can prevent them from pulling down the vines. You can use old stockings, fabric strips, or commercially available netting to create slings that cradle the fruit and distribute its weight evenly.

Pollination is critical for melons to set fruit, as these plants rely on pollinators like bees to transfer pollen from male to female flowers. To encourage pollinators, plant companion flowers such as marigolds, zinnias, and sunflowers near your melon patch. These flowers attract bees and other beneficial insects, improving pollination rates. In cases where natural pollination is insufficient, hand-pollination can be a valuable technique. Use a small paintbrush or cotton swab to transfer pollen from the male flowers (which have thin stems) to the female flowers (which have a small swelling at the base, indicating the developing fruit). This method ensures that each flower receives enough pollen to produce a healthy fruit.

Identifying and addressing common issues with fruit set is also important. Sometimes, poor pollination can result in misshapen or underdeveloped fruits. Ensuring your garden is a welcoming environment for pollinators is the first step. Additionally, fluctuating temperatures can affect pollination and fruit set. If you experience a period of unusually hot or cold weather, consider using row covers to protect your plants and create a more stable microclimate. Proper irrigation is also crucial. Consistent watering, especially during flowering and fruit development, helps maintain healthy plants and supports fruit set. Aim to keep the soil evenly moist but not waterlogged. Overhead watering can wash away pollen and disrupt the pollination process, so water at the base of the plants instead.

Growing melons requires thoughtful soil preparation, careful planting, and ongoing care. By focusing on these aspects, you can enjoy a bountiful harvest of sweet, juicy melons.

5.3 GRAPEVINES (GRAPES, KIWI)

Grapevines and kiwis can transform your garden into a lush, fruitful oasis. Choosing the right varieties is critical for success. For grapes, cold-hardy varieties like 'Concord' or 'Frontenac' are excellent choices for cooler climates. These varieties are bred to withstand frost and shorter growing seasons. If disease resistance is a concern, opt for varieties like 'Reliance' or 'Mars,' which are known for their resilience against common grape diseases such as powdery mildew and black rot. For kiwis, hardy varieties like 'Arctic Beauty' or 'Anna' thrive in temperate climates and can even tolerate temperatures as low as -25°F. These kiwis produce smaller but equally delicious fruits compared to their tropical cousins.

When planting grapevines, proper spacing and trellising are essential. Space each vine about 6 to 8 feet apart to allow ample room for growth and air circulation. This spacing helps prevent disease and ensures each plant gets sufficient sunlight. Installing a sturdy trellis system early on is crucial. Grapevines are vigorous climbers and require strong support to grow vertically. Use materials like galvanized wire and wooden posts to create a durable structure. Plant grapevines at the same depth they were in their nursery pots, ensuring the root ball is well-covered with soil. For kiwis, plant them about 10 to 15 feet apart, as they can become quite expansive. Provide a strong support structure like a pergola or arbor to manage their vigorous growth. Timing is also key; plant bare-root grapevines and kiwis in early spring before new growth starts, while potted plants can be planted in spring or fall.

Maintaining grapevines and kiwis throughout the growing season involves consistent watering, pruning, and fertilization. Grapevines thrive in soil that remains consistently moist but not waterlogged. Water deeply once a week, adjusting for rainfall and temperature. Mulching around the base of the plants can help retain moisture and suppress weeds. Pruning is vital for promoting healthy growth and fruit production. For grapevines, prune in late winter or early spring, removing any dead or weak wood and cutting back last year's growth to two or three buds. This practice encourages the development of strong, fruit-bearing canes. Kiwis also benefit from annual pruning. In late winter, remove any dead or crossing branches and thin out the canopy to improve air circulation. Fertilize both grapevines and kiwis with organic fertilizers, such as compost or well-rotted manure, in early spring and again in mid-summer to support vigorous growth and abundant fruiting.

Pest and disease management is crucial for keeping your grapevines and kiwis healthy. Grapevines are susceptible to pests like spider mites and leafhoppers, which can be controlled with neem oil. Apply the oil in the early morning or late evening to minimize harm to beneficial insects. Fungal diseases such as powdery mildew can be managed with sulfur sprays, ensuring good air circulation and avoiding overhead watering. For kiwis, common pests include scale insects and aphids. Insecticidal soap can effectively control these pests when applied regularly. Fungal diseases are less common in kiwis but can still occur in humid conditions. Ensuring proper spacing and pruning helps mitigate this risk. Using netting to protect your fruits from birds is also advisable. Birds can quickly deplete your harvest, so drape bird netting over your plants, securing it to the ground to prevent birds from getting underneath.

By selecting the right varieties, planting with care, and maintaining a vigilant approach to watering, pruning, and pest management, you can cultivate a successful and rewarding crop of grapes and kiwis. These practices ensure your plants remain healthy and productive, providing you with delicious, homegrown fruits season after season.

5.4 TROPICAL FRUITS FOR TEMPERATE CLIMATES (PINEAPPLE, PASSIONFRUIT)

Growing tropical fruits like pineapples and passionfruit in temperate climates can be a fulfilling endeavor, provided you create the right conditions. Selecting sunny, sheltered locations is crucial. These plants thrive in full sun, needing at least six hours of direct sunlight each day. Sheltered spots protect them from cold winds and sudden temperature drops, which can stress tropical plants. Microclimates, or small areas within your garden that have different climatic conditions than the surrounding area, can be utilized to your advantage. For instance, planting near a south-facing wall can create a warmer microclimate that mimics tropical conditions. Greenhouses are another excellent option. They provide controlled environments where you can manage temperature, humidity, and light, ensuring your tropical fruits have the best possible growing conditions. Ensuring well-draining, fertile soil is also vital. Tropical fruits dislike waterlogged conditions, so amend your soil with plenty of organic matter like compost or well-rotted manure to improve drainage and fertility.

When it comes to planting tropical fruits, the details matter. For pineapples, plant the crowns of the fruit about two inches deep in the soil, ensuring that the base is well-covered, but the leaves remain above ground. Space them about 12 to 18 inches apart to allow for growth. Passionfruit vines need more room to spread, so plant them about 6 to 10 feet apart. Using containers can make temperature management easier, especially for pineapples. Containers allow you to move plants indoors during colder months or unexpected frosts. When transplanting young plants, handle them gently to avoid damaging the roots. Plant at the same depth they were growing in their pots, and water thoroughly to help settle the soil around the roots.

Maintaining tropical fruits throughout the growing season requires regular care. Keeping the soil consistently moist is crucial, as these plants have high water needs. Water deep once or twice a week, depending on rainfall and temperature, ensuring the soil remains evenly moist but not waterlogged. Mulching around the base of the plants helps retain moisture, suppress weeds, and maintain a stable soil temperature. Use organic mulches like straw, wood chips, or compost. Fertilization is also key. Use organic fertilizers like compost, fish emulsion, or seaweed extract to provide a steady supply of nutrients. Apply fertilizer in early spring and again in mid-summer to support vigorous growth and fruit production.

Pollination is essential for tropical fruits to set and develop properly. Encouraging pollinators like bees can significantly improve fruit set. Plant companion flowers such as marigolds, zinnias, and sunflowers around your tropical fruit plants to attract these beneficial insects. Hand-pollination can also be a valuable technique, especially if natural pollination is insufficient. For passionfruit, use a small paintbrush to transfer pollen from the male parts of the flower (anthers) to the female parts (stigma). This ensures that each flower receives enough pollen to produce a healthy fruit. Monitoring fruit sets and addressing any issues promptly is important. If you notice poor fruit set, it could be due to inadequate pollination or environmental stress. Ensure your plants are in optimal conditions and consider hand-pollination to boost fruit production.

By creating suitable growing conditions, following detailed planting guidelines, and maintaining consistent care, you can successfully grow tropical fruits like pineapples and passionfruit in temperate climates. These practices ensure your plants thrive, providing you with a rewarding harvest of exotic fruits.

Growing edible fruits like berry bushes, melons, grapevines, and tropical fruits enriches your garden with diverse flavors and vibrant colors. Understanding the specific needs of each fruit type and providing tailored care ensures a bountiful harvest. Next, we'll explore the world of non-fruit-bearing trees, flowers, and shrubs, adding beauty and structure to your garden.

CHAPTER 6
SOIL AND WATER MANAGEMENT

Understanding and managing soil pH can make the difference between a thriving garden and one that struggles. This chapter will guide you through the process of testing and improving your soil pH to create the optimal environment for your plants.

6.1 TESTING AND IMPROVING SOIL PH

Understanding soil pH is fundamental to successful gardening. Soil pH measures the acidity or alkalinity of the soil, which directly impacts nutrient availability and plant health. On the pH scale, which ranges from 0 to 14, a value of 7 is neutral. Values below 7 indicate acidity, while those above 7 indicate alkalinity. Most garden plants prefer a slightly acidic to neutral pH, typically between 6.0 and 7.0. This range ensures that essential nutrients like nitrogen, phosphorus, and potassium are readily available for plant uptake. Acid-loving plants, such as blueberries and azaleas, thrive in soil with a pH between 4.5 and 5.5. Conversely, plants like lilacs and lavender prefer slightly alkaline conditions, with a pH between 7.0 and 8.0. Signs of pH imbalance in your garden include yellowing leaves, poor growth, and nutrient deficiencies, which can often be mistaken for other issues.

Testing your soil pH accurately is the first step in addressing these imbalances. Start by collecting soil samples from various parts of your garden. Use a clean trowel to dig 4 to 6 inches below the surface and gather at least 2 cups of soil. Mix the samples together in a clean container, breaking up clumps and removing debris. You can test the soil pH using a pH test kit or strips, which are readily available at garden centers. Alternatively, you can use the baking soda and vinegar method for a quick, home-based test. For this method, mix one part soil with two parts distilled water to create a slurry. Add either vinegar or baking soda to the mixture. If it fizzes with vinegar, the soil is alkaline; if it fizzes with baking soda, the soil is acidic. While this method is less precise, it gives a general idea of your soil's pH. For more accurate results, consider using a soil pH meter or sending samples to a professional lab.

Once you have your test results, you can take steps to adjust your soil pH as needed. To raise the pH of acidic soil, add lime (calcium carbonate). The amount of lime required depends on the current pH and the soil type. Sandy soils require less lime than clay soils to achieve the same pH change. Apply lime evenly over the soil surface and work it into the top 6 inches of soil. It's best to do this in the fall, allowing the lime to react with the soil over the winter. To lower the pH of alkaline soil, use sulfur or aluminum sulfate. Sulfur is slower-acting but longer-lasting, while aluminum sulfate works more quickly. As with lime, the amount needed varies based on the soil type and current pH. Work the sulfur or aluminum sulfate into the soil in the spring or fall for the best results. Incorporating organic matter, such as compost or peat moss, can also help buffer pH changes and improve soil structure.

Ongoing monitoring and maintenance of soil pH are essential for long-term plant health. Regularly testing your soil, at least once a year, allows you to track changes and adjust as needed. Pay attention to your plants' performance and watch for signs of pH imbalance, such as yellowing leaves or stunted growth. Adjust the pH based on these observations and test results. For example, if you notice that your acid-loving plants are not thriving despite adequate care, it may be time to lower the pH by adding sulfur. Additionally, using pH-adjusted water for irrigation can help maintain the desired soil pH. If your tap water is highly alkaline, consider using rainwater or adding a mild acid, such as vinegar, to your irrigation water to keep the pH balanced.

Soil pH Testing Checklist

- Collect soil samples from various garden areas.
- Use a clean trowel to dig 4-6 inches below the surface.
- Combine samples in a clean container, breaking up clumps and removing debris.
- Test the soil using a pH test kit, strips, or a pH meter.

- Interpret the results to determine if adjustments are needed.

Regularly testing and adjusting your soil pH ensures that your plants have access to the nutrients they need to thrive. By understanding the importance of soil pH and taking proactive steps to manage it, you create a foundation for a healthy, productive garden.

6.2 EFFICIENT WATERING TECHNIQUES

Watering your garden correctly is crucial for plant health and growth. Different plants have varying water needs, and understanding these needs helps you maintain a thriving garden. Some plants, like leafy greens, require consistent moisture, while others, like succulents, need less frequent watering. The type of soil in your garden also plays a significant role in water retention. Sandy soils drain quickly and may need more frequent watering, whereas clay soils retain water longer but can become waterlogged. Understanding your soil type can guide you in adjusting your watering practices to ensure your plants get the right amount of moisture. Deep watering is generally more effective than shallow watering. It encourages roots to grow deeper into the soil, making plants more drought resistant. Shallow watering, on the other hand, can lead to weak root systems and plants that are more susceptible to stress.

Watering frequency and timing are key to optimizing plant growth. Watering early in the morning or late in the evening is ideal. During these times, temperatures are cooler, and evaporation rates are lower, allowing more water to reach the roots. Adjust your watering schedule based on weather conditions. On hot, dry days, you may need to water more frequently. Conversely, during cooler or rainy periods, you can reduce the frequency. Seasonal variations also affect watering needs. In the spring and fall, when temperatures are moderate, plants may require less water. During the peak of summer, when temperatures soar, you might need to increase the frequency to keep the soil consistently moist.

Efficient watering techniques can help you use water wisely while ensuring your plants thrive. Soaker hoses are an excellent option for targeted irrigation. They deliver water directly to the soil, minimizing evaporation and ensuring that it reaches the root zone. Implementing a watering schedule can help minimize waste. Set specific times for watering and stick to them, adjusting as needed based on the weather and the specific needs of your plants. Grouping plants with similar water needs together can also make watering more efficient. This practice, known as hydrozoning, allows you to tailor your watering practices to the needs of different plant groups. For example, group drought-tolerant plants like lavender and succulents together, while placing water-loving plants like tomatoes and cucumbers in another area.

Conserving water in the garden is not only environmentally responsible but also beneficial for plant health. Installing rain barrels is an effective way to collect and store rainwater for garden use. Place barrels under downspouts to capture runoff from your roof. This free water source can be used during dry spells, reducing your reliance on municipal water supplies. Greywater systems, which recycle water from household activities like washing dishes and laundry, can also be used for irrigation. Ensure that the greywater is free from harmful chemicals and detergents before using it on your plants. Reducing evaporation is another critical aspect of water conservation. Applying mulch around your plants helps retain soil moisture, keep the soil cool, and reduce weed growth. Organic mulches like straw, wood chips, and compost are particularly effective. Ground covers, such as low-growing plants or creeping perennials, can also help reduce evaporation by shading the soil and retaining moisture.

Efficient watering techniques and water conservation practices are essential for maintaining a healthy garden. By understanding your plants' water needs and adjusting your watering practices accordingly, you can ensure that your garden thrives. Use soaker hoses for targeted irrigation, stick to a watering schedule, and group plants with similar water needs together. Install rain barrels to collect rainwater, use greywater systems, and apply mulch or ground covers to reduce evaporation. These practices not only help you use water wisely but also contribute to a more sustainable and productive garden.

6.3 DRIP IRRIGATION SYSTEMS

One of the most efficient ways to water your garden is through a drip irrigation system. This method offers numerous benefits, starting with its ability to reduce water waste. By delivering water directly to the plant roots, drip irrigation minimizes evaporation and runoff. This targeted application ensures that each plant gets the precise amount of water it needs, conserving water while promoting healthy growth. Moreover, since the foliage remains dry, the risk of diseases caused by wet leaves is significantly lower. This not only keeps your plants healthier but also reduces the need for chemical treatments. Additionally, drip irrigation improves water penetration to the root zones, encouraging deeper root growth. This results in stronger, more resilient plants capable of withstanding drought conditions better than those watered by traditional methods.

Planning and designing a drip irrigation system requires careful consideration of your garden layout, and the specific water needs of your plants. Start by assessing the size and shape of your garden, noting the location of different plant groups. This will help you determine the length of tubing and the number of emitters required. Next, choose the right components for your system. Emitters, which release water at a controlled rate, come in various flow rates, so select the ones best suited to your plants' needs. Tubing and connectors are also essential; these should be durable and UV-resistant to withstand outdoor conditions. Once you have your components, create a system layout plan. Sketch your garden, marking the mainline, lateral lines, and the placement of emitters. This plan will serve as a blueprint during installation, ensuring that every part of your garden receives adequate water.

The installation process of a drip irrigation system begins with laying out and securing the tubing. Start by unrolling the mainline tubing along the central path of your garden. Use stakes to secure it in place, ensuring it lies flat and straight. Next, install the lateral lines branching off the mainline, positioning them near the plant rows or beds. Attach the emitters to the lateral lines, spacing them according to your plants' water requirements. For instance, place emitters closer together for densely planted areas and further apart for widely spaced plants. Once the emitters are in place, connect the system to a water source. This can be a garden hose, faucet, or rain barrel equipped with a filter to prevent debris from clogging the emitters. Finally, test the system for leaks and proper function. Turn on the water and check for any issues, adjusting the emitters or connectors as needed to ensure even water distribution.

Maintaining and troubleshooting your drip irrigation system is crucial for its long-term effectiveness. Regularly check for clogs and leaks, especially at the emitters, as these can disrupt water flow and reduce efficiency. Flushing the system periodically helps remove any debris that may have accumulated in the lines. Simply disconnect the end caps and let the water run through the tubing for a few minutes. Adjusting the placement of emitters as plants grow ensures they continue to receive adequate water. For instance, as a shrub expands, move the emitters to the outer edge of the root zone to encourage wider root development. Seasonal maintenance tasks, such as winterizing the system, are also essential. In colder climates, remove and store any removable parts, and drain the tubing to prevent damage from freezing temperatures.

Drip irrigation is a smart and sustainable way to water your garden, offering numerous benefits for both plant health and water conservation. By carefully planning, installing, and maintaining your system, you can ensure that your garden thrives with minimal water waste and reduced disease risk. Whether you have a small backyard plot or an extensive vegetable garden, drip irrigation can provide the precise, efficient watering your plants need to flourish.

6.4 MULCHING FOR MOISTURE RETENTION

Mulching is a simple yet powerful technique that can greatly enhance your garden's health and productivity. There are various types of mulch, each offering unique benefits for moisture retention. Organic mulches, such as straw, wood chips, and compost, are particularly effective. Straw is lightweight and easy to spread, making it a great choice for vegetable gardens. It decomposes slowly, providing long-term moisture retention and weed suppression. Wood chips, on the other hand, are ideal for perennial beds and around trees. They break down over time, adding valuable organic matter to the soil. Compost, rich in nutrients, not only retains moisture but also enriches the soil, promoting healthy plant growth. Inorganic mulches, such as gravel and landscape fabric, offer different advantages. Gravel is excellent for pathways and areas where you want to prevent weed growth without adding organic matter. It allows water to permeate while reducing evaporation. Landscape fabric, used under a layer of organic mulch, provides a long-lasting barrier against weeds and helps retain soil moisture.

Applying mulch effectively requires attention to detail. Start by spreading a layer of mulch around your plants, ensuring it is thick enough to retain moisture but not so thick that it smothers the plants. For most organic mulches, a depth of 2 to 4 inches is ideal. Coarser mulches like wood chips can be applied more thickly, up to 6 inches. When mulching around plants, leave a small gap around the base to prevent moisture buildup and potential rot. This is especially important for trees and shrubs, where mulch piled against the trunk can lead to decay. Timing is also crucial. Apply mulch in the spring after the soil has warmed up to help retain moisture and suppress weeds throughout the growing season. In the fall, add a fresh layer to protect the soil and plant roots during the winter months.

Beyond moisture retention, mulching offers numerous other benefits. One of the most significant is weed suppression. A thick layer of mulch blocks sunlight, preventing weed seeds from germinating and reducing the need for manual weeding. Mulch also helps regulate soil temperature, keeping it cooler in the summer and warmer in the winter. This temperature regulation creates a more stable environment for plant roots, promoting healthier growth. As organic mulch decomposes, it adds valuable organic matter to the soil. This improves soil structure, enhances nutrient availability, and supports beneficial soil organisms. Mulching can also reduce soil erosion by protecting the soil surface from heavy rains and wind, maintaining soil integrity and preventing nutrient loss.

Maintaining mulch layers throughout the growing season is essential for maximizing their benefits. Over time, organic mulches break down and thin out, reducing their effectiveness. Replenish mulch as needed to maintain the desired depth, usually once or twice a year. Avoid allowing mulch to build up against plant stems or trunks, as this can lead to rot and disease. Instead, gently pull mulch back from the base of plants, creating a small ring of bare soil. Seasonal adjustments to mulch depth can also enhance its effectiveness. In the summer, a thicker layer of mulch helps retain moisture and keep the soil cool. In the winter, adding a fresh layer of mulch provides extra insulation, protecting plant roots from freezing temperatures. Regularly inspect your mulch layers and adjust based on the season and the specific needs of your plants.

Mulching is a versatile and beneficial practice that can significantly improve your garden's health and productivity. By choosing the right type of mulch, applying it correctly, and maintaining it throughout the season, you create a more stable and supportive environment for your plants. This simple technique not only conserves water and suppresses weeds but also enhances soil health and promotes robust plant growth.

In the next chapter, we'll delve into pest management strategies, providing you with the tools and knowledge to protect your garden from common threats and ensure a bountiful harvest.

YOUR FEEDBACK IS VALUED!

Thank you for reading *The Grinning Gardener's Handbook Volume 1: A Comprehensive Guide to Growing Amazing Organic Fruits and Vegetables in Different Climates and Seasons*. I hope this book has inspired you and provided valuable insights to help you cultivate a thriving organic garden, no matter where you live.

If you found this book helpful, I'd be so grateful if you could take a moment to leave a **5-star** review on Amazon.

★★★★★

It costs nothing, but your review can make a world of difference in helping others, just like you, find this book. Every review not only supports my work but also increases the chances that this message will reach more people. Your thoughts on how *The Grinning Gardener's Handbook* helped you, what you liked most, or even areas where you'd like more information in future volumes, will help us create even better resources for gardeners like you.

How to Leave a Review:

1. Visit the book's page on Amazon.
2. Scroll down to the "Customer Reviews" section.
3. Click "Write a customer review" and share your thoughts!

Happy gardening!

—The Grinning Gardener 🌿

CHAPTER 7
PEST AND DISEASE CONTROL

Integrated Pest Management (IPM) is a holistic approach to pest control that can transform your gardening practices. This chapter will guide you through the principles and practices of

IPM, helping you manage pests effectively while minimizing chemical use.

7.1 INTEGRATED PEST MANAGEMENT (IPM) BASICS

Integrated Pest Management (IPM) is an ecosystem-based strategy that focuses on long-term prevention and control of pests through a combination of techniques. The goal of IPM is to minimize pest damage while reducing reliance on chemical pesticides. By understanding the life cycles of pests and their interactions with the environment, you can employ a variety of methods to keep pest populations under control. IPM is not about eradicating pests entirely but managing them in a way that keeps their numbers at acceptable levels. This approach emphasizes the importance of monitoring and early detection to address pest problems before they become severe.

The four-tiered approach of IPM is a comprehensive framework that guides you through effective pest management.

Prevention

This is the first and most crucial tier. By creating a healthy growing environment, you can reduce the likelihood of pest infestations. This includes practices like crop rotation to disrupt pest life cycles and planting resistant varieties that are less susceptible to pests. Proper plant spacing is vital for air circulation, which helps prevent the buildup of moisture that attracts pests. Using row covers can protect seedlings from insect damage, allowing them to establish strong roots before facing potential threats.

Monitoring

Monitoring is the second tier and involves regular inspections of your garden. This means checking your plants frequently, especially the undersides of leaves where pests often hide. By identifying pest thresholds, you can determine when action is needed. A zero-tolerance approach to pests is unrealistic; instead, establish an action threshold that allows for some pest presence without significant damage. Regular monitoring helps you catch problems early, making them easier to manage with less intervention.

Control

Incorporating mechanical, biological, and cultural methods, the third tier focuses on control. Mechanical controls involve physical removal of pests, such as hand-picking or using high-pressure water sprays to dislodge insects like aphids. Traps, such as sticky traps for flying insects or live traps for rodents, can also be effective. Biological controls use natural predators and beneficial insects to keep pest populations in check. Introducing ladybugs, lacewings, or parasitic wasps can reduce aphid numbers and other pests. Cultural controls focus on creating an environment that is less hospitable to pests. This includes practices like maintaining healthy soil, using proper watering techniques, and ensuring good ventilation in your garden.

Evaluation

The final tier is evaluation, which involves assessing the effectiveness of your pest management strategies. After implementing control measures, observe your garden to see if pest levels are reduced and plant health improves. If a particular method is not working, be prepared to adjust your approach. Continuous learning and adaptation are key components of successful IPM. By evaluating your results and making necessary changes, you can refine your pest management practices and achieve better outcomes over time.

Cultural practices play a significant role in preventing pest problems. Proper plant spacing ensures good air circulation, reducing the risk of fungal diseases and deterring pests that thrive in humid conditions. Crop rotation is another essential practice. By rotating crops from different plant families, you disrupt the life cycles of pests and reduce the buildup of soil-borne diseases. For example, planting legumes one year and brassicas the next can help break pest and disease cycles. Using row covers to protect seedlings is another effective cultural control. These lightweight fabrics shield young plants from insects while allowing light, air, and moisture to reach them. Once the plants are established and stronger, the covers can be removed.

Real-life examples of successful IPM implementation highlight the effectiveness of this approach. In one case, a gardener used trap crops to divert pests from valuable plants. By planting radishes around a bed of lettuce, the radishes attracted flea beetles, sparing the lettuce from damage. Another gardener introduced beneficial insects like ladybugs to control an aphid infestation on their roses. The ladybugs quickly reduced the aphid population, allowing the roses to recover without the use of chemical pesticides. Implementing crop diversity is another successful strategy. A diverse garden with a mix of flowers, vegetables, and herbs can reduce pest outbreaks by creating a more balanced ecosystem. For example, planting marigolds alongside tomatoes can repel nematodes and other pests, while attracting beneficial insects that help control aphids and whiteflies.

By embracing the principles and practices of IPM, you can create a healthier, more resilient garden. This approach not only reduces the need for chemical interventions but also promotes a balanced ecosystem where plants, pests, and beneficial organisms coexist. Through prevention, monitoring, control, and evaluation, you can manage pests effectively and enjoy a thriving garden.

7.2 NATURAL PEST REPELLENTS

Gardening can sometimes feel like a battleground, with pests constantly trying to invade your green sanctuary. But there's no need to reach for harsh chemicals when you have a pantry full of natural solutions. Homemade pest repellents can be both effective and gentle on the environment. One such remedy is garlic spray, which works wonders against aphids and caterpillars. To make it, simply blend two bulbs of garlic with a quart of water, strain the mixture, and add a teaspoon of mild dish soap. Spray this concoction on your plants, focusing on the undersides of leaves where pests like to hide. The strong smell of garlic deters many insects, keeping your plants safe and healthy.

Neem oil spray is another versatile option that targets a broad spectrum of pests, from aphids and spider mites to whiteflies and mealybugs. Neem oil, derived from the seeds of the neem tree, disrupts the life cycle of insects, making it harder for them to grow and reproduce. Mix two teaspoons of neem oil with a quart of water and a few drops of dish soap, then spray it on your plants every two weeks. This natural insecticide not only keeps pests at bay but also has antifungal properties, helping to prevent diseases like powdery mildew.

For soft-bodied insects like aphids, scale, and thrips, a simple soap spray can be highly effective. Combine one tablespoon of liquid soap with a quart of water and spray it directly on the insects. The soap breaks down their outer protective layer, causing them to dehydrate and die. Be sure to use a soap that is free from additives and fragrances, as these can harm your plants. Test the spray on a small area first to ensure your plants are not sensitive to it.

Certain plants naturally repel pests when grown alongside susceptible crops, creating a harmonious and pest-resistant garden. Marigolds, for instance, are known to deter nematodes, tiny worms that attack plant roots. Their roots release a substance that repels these pests, making them an excellent companion for tomatoes, peppers, and other vegetables. Basil is another powerhouse in the garden, repelling mosquitoes and flies. Plant it near your tomatoes and peppers to keep these annoying insects away while enhancing the flavor of the vegetables. Nasturtiums, with their vibrant flowers, attract aphids away from more valuable plants, acting as a trap crop. By planting nasturtiums around your garden, you can lure aphids away from your prized roses and vegetables, reducing the overall pest pressure.

Essential oils and plant extracts offer another layer of natural pest control. Peppermint oil is particularly effective against ants and spiders. Dilute a few drops of peppermint oil in a spray bottle filled with water and apply it around your garden and home to create a barrier that these pests will avoid. Rosemary oil works well against flea beetles and cabbage moths. Mix a teaspoon of rosemary oil with water and spray it on your plants to keep these pests at bay. Citrus oil, derived from the peels of oranges and lemons, can repel mites and aphids. Its strong scent confuses and deters these pests, protecting your plants from infestations.

Physical barriers can also play a crucial role in protecting your plants from pests. Floating row covers are lightweight fabrics that can be draped over plants to shield them from insects while allowing light, air, and moisture to pass through. These covers are especially useful for protecting seedlings and young plants from pests like flea beetles and cabbage worms. Copper tape is an effective deterrent for slugs and snails. When these pests encounter the tape, it creates a mild electric charge that repels them. Place copper tape around the base of plant pots or along garden beds to keep slugs and snails at bay. Sticky traps are another simple yet effective tool for monitoring and reducing flying insect populations. These traps, coated with a sticky substance, capture insects like whiteflies, fungus gnats, and aphids, preventing them from laying eggs and spreading throughout your garden.

Incorporating these natural pest repellents into your gardening routine can significantly reduce pest problems without harming the environment. By using homemade sprays, planting pest-repellent plants, applying essential oils, and utilizing physical barriers, you create a garden that is both productive and resilient. These methods not only protect your plants but also contribute to a healthier ecosystem, where beneficial insects and natural predators can thrive.

7.3 BENEFICIAL INSECTS AND POLLINATORS

Ladybugs, or lady beetles, play a crucial role in keeping aphid populations under control, preventing these pests from damaging your plants. Their presence in your garden is a sign of a healthy, balanced ecosystem.

Lacewings are another valuable ally in the garden. These delicate insects, with their transparent wings and golden eyes, may seem fragile, but their larvae are fierce predators. Lacewing larvae, often called "aphid lions," feed on a variety of pests, including aphids, caterpillars, and whiteflies. They are particularly effective in managing soft-bodied insects that can cause significant damage to your plants. The adult lacewings, which feed on nectar and pollen, also contribute to pollination, making them a dual-purpose insect in your garden.

Predatory beetles, such as ground beetles and soldier beetles, are essential for controlling soil-dwelling pests. Ground beetles are swift hunters that patrol the soil surface, preying on pests like slugs, snails, and root maggots. Soldier beetles, with their bright orange or yellow bodies, are often seen on flowers, where they feed on nectar and pollen. Their larvae, however, are formidable predators of soil-dwelling pests, including caterpillars and beetle larvae. By introducing and maintaining populations of these beneficial beetles, you can significantly reduce pest problems in your garden.

Attracting and maintaining populations of beneficial insects requires thoughtful planning and a welcoming environment. Planting nectar and pollen-rich flowers is one of the most effective strategies. Flowers like yarrow, dill, fennel, and cosmos provide the necessary food sources for adult beneficial insects. These plants not only attract beneficial insects but also add beauty and diversity to your garden. Creating insect habitats, such as bug hotels, can offer shelter and nesting sites for beneficial insects. Bug hotels, made from natural materials like bamboo, straw, and wood, provide a safe haven for insects to reproduce and overwinter.

Avoiding broad-spectrum pesticides is crucial for protecting beneficial insect populations. These pesticides do not discriminate between harmful pests and beneficial insects, wiping out both and disrupting the natural balance in your garden. Instead, focus on targeted pest control methods that minimize harm to beneficial insects. By fostering a garden environment that supports beneficial insects, you create a resilient ecosystem that can naturally manage pest populations.

Pollinators are the unsung heroes of fruit and vegetable production. Bees, butterflies, and other pollinators play a vital role in the reproduction of many plants, transferring pollen from flower to flower and enabling fruit set. Without pollinators, many of the fruits and vegetables we rely on would fail to produce. Bees are essential pollinators for crops like apples, tomatoes, and cucumbers. Butterflies, with their vibrant wings, not only add beauty to your garden but also contribute to pollination as they flit from flower to flower.

To support these crucial pollinators, plant pollinator-friendly plants like lavender, sunflowers, and coneflowers. These plants provide nectar and pollen, the primary food sources for pollinators. Incorporating a variety of flowering plants with staggered bloom times ensures a continuous supply of food throughout the growing season. Early blooming plants like crocuses and late-blooming plants like asters provide nectar and pollen when other flowers are scarce.

Providing water sources for pollinators is another important consideration. A shallow dish filled with water and pebbles can serve as a drinking spot for bees and butterflies. The pebbles give them a place to land and drink without the risk of drowning. Placing these water sources in sunny, sheltered spots in your garden makes them easily accessible to pollinators.

Designing a pollinator-friendly garden involves creating a diverse and supportive environment. Incorporate a variety of flowering plants with different shapes, colors, and bloom times to attract a wide range of pollinators. Providing nesting sites for bees, such as bee houses or bare patches of soil, encourages solitary bees to make your garden their home. Reducing pesticide use is essential for protecting pollinators. Many pesticides are harmful to bees and butterflies, so opt for natural pest control methods whenever possible. By creating a welcoming habitat for pollinators, you not only enhance your garden's productivity but also contribute to the health and diversity of the local ecosystem.

7.4 MANAGING COMMON PLANT DISEASES

Preventing plant diseases involves several proactive strategies that can save you from future headaches. Crop rotation is a key practice to avoid disease buildup in your soil. By changing the types of plants you grow in each area of your garden every year, you disrupt the life cycles of pathogens that target specific plant families. For instance, if you plant tomatoes in one spot this year, consider planting beans or another unrelated crop in the same spot next year. This simple practice can dramatically reduce the incidence of soil-borne diseases and keep your garden healthier over time.

Proper spacing of plants is another critical factor in disease prevention. Crowded plants create a humid environment, which is a breeding ground for many diseases. Adequate spacing ensures good air circulation, helping to keep the foliage dry and less susceptible to fungal infections. When planting, follow the spacing recommendations for each type of plant to give them room to breathe and grow.

Watering practices also play a significant role in disease prevention. Watering at the base of plants rather than overhead helps keep the foliage dry. Wet leaves are more prone to fungal diseases, so using a soaker hose or drip irrigation system can be particularly effective. Watering early in the morning allows any moisture on the leaves to evaporate quickly as the day warms up, reducing the risk of disease.

Identifying plant diseases early can make a big difference in managing them effectively. Powdery mildew is a common fungal disease that appears as white, powdery spots on the leaves, stems, and flowers. It thrives in warm, dry conditions and can spread quickly. To combat powdery mildew, use baking soda spray. Mix one tablespoon of baking soda with a gallon of water, add a few drops of dish soap, and spray it on the affected plants. This solution can help prevent the spread of the disease and protect your plants.

Blight is another serious disease that affects many plants, including tomatoes and potatoes. It appears as dark, water-soaked spots on the leaves and stems, often leading to plant collapse. Early blight typically starts on older leaves, while late blight can affect the entire plant rapidly. Managing blight involves removing and destroying infected plant material to prevent the disease from spreading. Copper fungicides can also be effective in controlling blight. Apply the fungicide according to the manufacturer's instructions, focusing on the lower leaves and stems where the disease often begins.

Rust is a fungal disease that manifests as orange or brown pustules on the undersides of leaves. It can weaken plants and reduce their productivity. Removing and disposing of infected leaves is crucial to managing rust. Ensure you do not compost the infected material, as this can spread the disease. Maintaining good garden hygiene by cleaning up plant debris and rotating crops can help prevent rust from taking hold.

Choosing disease-resistant plant varieties can also make your gardening efforts more successful. For example, select tomato varieties that are resistant to blight, such as 'Mountain Magic' or 'Defiant'. These varieties have been bred to withstand the disease, reducing the need for chemical treatments. Similarly, squash varieties like 'Sunshine' or 'Sunglo' are resistant to powdery mildew, making them easier to grow in humid conditions. For beans, opt for rust-resistant varieties like 'Provider' or 'Roma II'. These disease-resistant plants can significantly reduce the incidence of problems in your garden, allowing you to enjoy a healthier and more productive harvest.

By focusing on disease prevention strategies, early identification, and choosing resistant varieties, you can manage common plant diseases effectively. This approach not only protects your plants but also enhances the overall health and resilience of your garden. Understanding these practices helps create a thriving garden environment where plants can flourish with minimal intervention.

CHAPTER 8
ADVANCED GARDENING TECHNIQUES

Grafting is a technique that can breathe new life into aging trees and create fruit trees with superior qualities. This chapter will guide you through the intricacies of grafting, providing you with the knowledge and confidence to master this ancient art.

8.1 GRAFTING FOR FRUIT PLANTS

Grafting is a technique that involves joining parts from two different plants so they grow as one. The primary purpose of grafting is to combine the desirable traits of two plants. For instance, you might graft a fruit-bearing scion, which is the upper part of the graft with dormant buds, onto a rootstock that has superior root system qualities. This method is invaluable for plants that do not root well from cuttings or for maintaining the genetic identity of a particular variety. Grafting can significantly improve disease resistance and enhance fruit quality. Common grafting methods include cleft grafting, where a scion is inserted into a cleft in the rootstock, and whip and tongue grafting, which involves interlocking cuts on both scion and rootstock for a stronger union.

Selecting the right rootstock and scion is crucial for successful grafting. A good rootstock should be disease-resistant, hardy, and well-adapted to your soil and climate conditions. Rootstocks influence the size, vigor, and overall health of the grafted plant. The scion, on the other hand, should come from a healthy, productive plant known for its desirable fruit qualities. It's important to ensure compatibility between the rootstock and scion, as not all combinations will result in successful grafts. For example, apple scions graft well onto apple rootstocks, but they would not be compatible with cherry rootstocks. Timing is also critical; collecting scion wood during the plant's dormant season, typically in winter or early spring, ensures that the buds are ready to grow once grafted.

The grafting process begins with preparing both the rootstock and the scion. Start by making a clean, angled cut on the rootstock where you intend to attach the scion. The cut should be smooth to ensure good contact between the two parts. Next, prepare the scion by making a corresponding cut that matches the rootstock. Precision is key here; the cuts must align perfectly to ensure the cambium layers of both parts meet. This layer, located just beneath the bark, is where new growth occurs. Once the cuts are made, join the scion and rootstock, securing them with grafting tape or wax. This not only holds the graft in place but also prevents moisture loss and protects against infection. Aftercare is essential for graft success. Keep the grafted plant in a sheltered location, away from strong winds and direct sunlight, and maintain consistent moisture levels. Regularly check for signs of growth and remove any shoots that emerge from below the graft union to ensure the scion receives all the nutrients.

Grafting can present challenges, and troubleshooting common issues is part of the learning process. Graft failure often results from poor technique or environmental stress. If the graft union fails to take, reassess your cutting and alignment methods. Using sharp, sterilized tools can make a significant difference. Infection at the graft site is another common problem. This can be mitigated by ensuring a clean working environment and using protective grafting wax. Mismatched grafts, where the scion and rootstock are not compatible, will not grow successfully. In such cases, revisiting the compatibility of your chosen plants is necessary. Learning from these setbacks will improve your grafting skills over time.

Grafting Success Checklist

- Select disease-resistant rootstock and healthy scion wood.
- Ensure compatibility between rootstock and scion.
- Make clean, precise cuts for perfect alignment.
- Secure the graft with tape or wax.
- Provide aftercare by sheltering the plant and maintaining moisture.
- Troubleshoot issues like graft failure and infections diligently.

By mastering grafting techniques, you can unlock a world of possibilities in your garden, creating robust, productive fruit trees that combine the best traits of different plants. This skill not only enhances your garden's productivity but also preserves heirloom varieties and improves plant resilience.

8.2 SOIL BLOCKING FOR SEED STARTING

One of the most satisfying aspects of gardening is watching tiny seeds sprout into robust seedlings, ready to take on the world. Soil blocking, a method of starting seeds in cubes of compressed soil, offers several advantages that can make this process even more rewarding. One major benefit is the reduction of transplant shock. When you transfer plants grown in plastic pots, their roots often experience stress. Soil blocks, however, allow roots to grow naturally, reducing the risk of damage during transplanting. This method also promotes improved root development. As roots reach the edge of the block, they naturally air prune, encouraging a dense, fibrous root system. Soil blocking eliminates the need for plastic pots, making it an eco-friendly option. Moreover, it gives you greater control over soil composition, allowing you to tailor the mix to the specific needs of your plants.

Creating soil blocks is straightforward but requires attention to detail. Start by mixing the right soil blend. A blend of peat, compost, soil, and sand or perlite works well. The mix should be moist but not waterlogged, with a consistency like wet concrete. Using a soil blocker tool, compress the mix firmly into uniform blocks. Press the blocker into the soil mix, then scrape off the excess soil. Release the blocks onto a tray by pressing the handle, ensuring they hold their shape. Adjusting soil moisture is crucial. Too dry, and the blocks will crumble; too wet, and they won't hold together. Aim for a balance that allows the blocks to retain their shape while providing enough moisture for seed germination.

Sowing seeds in soil blocks involves a few simple steps. Choose seeds that are well-suited for soil blocking, such as tomatoes, peppers, and herbs. Plant each seed at the appropriate depth, usually about twice the seed's diameter, and press it gently into the block. Space the seeds evenly within each block to ensure they have room to grow. Label each block with the seed type and planting date for easy identification. Organize the blocks on a tray, and place them in a warm, well-lit area. Consistent labeling and organization will help you keep track of your seedlings and ensure you're providing the right care for each type.

Caring for soil blocks involves regular attention to watering, lighting, and monitoring for pests and diseases. Soil blocks should be kept moist but not waterlogged. Bottom-watering works best, as it allows the blocks to absorb water from the tray, reducing the risk of crumbling. Ensure the blocks are in a location with adequate light. If natural sunlight is insufficient, use grow lights to provide the necessary illumination. Monitor the seedlings daily for any signs of pests or diseases. Common issues include aphids and damping-off, a fungal disease that causes seedlings to collapse. Address these problems promptly by removing affected plants and using organic treatments like neem oil or insecticidal soap.

Soil Blocking Success Checklist

- Mix the right soil blend: peat, compost, soil, and sand or perlite.
- Compress soil into uniform blocks using a soil blocker tool.
- Ensure soil moisture is balanced for optimal block formation.
- Choose seeds suitable for soil blocking, such as tomatoes and herbs.
- Plant seeds at the appropriate depth and space them evenly.
- Label and organize blocks for easy identification.
- Use bottom-watering to keep blocks moist without waterlogging.
- Provide adequate light, using grow lights if necessary.
- Monitor pests and diseases, and address issues promptly.

By incorporating soil blocking into your seed-starting routine, you can enjoy healthier seedlings, reduced transplant shock, and a more sustainable gardening practice. The benefits of this method extend beyond the initial stages of plant growth, setting the foundation for robust plants that will thrive in your garden.

8.3 VERTICAL GARDENING SOLUTIONS

Vertical gardening involves growing plants upward instead of outward, making it ideal for small spaces like balconies, patios, and urban gardens. This technique offers numerous advantages, including better air circulation, reduced pest problems, and easier maintenance. Plants suitable for vertical growth include climbing vegetables like cucumbers and pole beans, fruits such as grapes and kiwi, and ornamental flowers like climbing roses and honeysuckle. Vertical gardening transforms limited spaces into lush, productive gardens.

Different vertical gardening systems cater to various needs and preferences. Trellises and arbors are classic choices for supporting climbing plants. Trellises can be simple structures made of wood or metal, while arbors provide a more decorative element. Both support plants like tomatoes, peas, and flowering vines, allowing them to grow upward and save ground space. Wall-mounted planters are perfect for herbs and small vegetables. These planters attach directly to walls, creating a living wall that's both functional and aesthetically pleasing. Hydroponic vertical towers offer an efficient way to grow plants using nutrient-rich water instead of soil. These systems are ideal for urban gardeners with limited access to traditional gardening spaces. Green walls, which involve growing plants on vertical surfaces, can serve both decorative and functional purposes. They improve air quality, reduce ambient temperatures, and add a touch of nature to urban environments.

Designing a vertical garden requires careful planning to ensure success. Start by choosing the right location with adequate sunlight, as most plants need at least six hours of direct light daily. Assess the strength and stability of the structures you'll use, whether they're freestanding or attached to a wall. Materials like wood, metal, and plastic can all be used, but ensure they can support the weight of mature plants. Plan your plant placement for optimal growth and aesthetics. Place taller plants at the bottom and shorter ones at the top to ensure all receive sufficient light. Consider the growth habits of your chosen plants. Fast-growing climbers might need more robust support, while smaller plants can thrive in simpler setups.

Maintaining vertical gardens involves specific techniques to ensure healthy plant development. Watering is crucial, as vertical setups can dry out faster than traditional gardens. Drip irrigation systems work well for vertical gardens, delivering water directly to the roots. Alternatively, hand-watering with a long-spout watering can ensure even distribution. Pruning and training plants are essential to manage growth and prevent overcrowding. Regularly trim back excessive growth and guide vines along their supports to maintain an orderly appearance. Monitoring for pests and diseases is also vital. Vertical gardens can sometimes create hidden pockets where pests thrive. Regular inspections and prompt treatment with organic solutions like neem oil or insecticidal soap keep problems at bay.

Imagine setting up a trellis against a sunny wall, planting peas at the base, and watching them climb and flourish. The vertical space not only adds beauty to your garden but also provides a practical solution for limited areas. As the peas grow, you guide their tendrils along the trellis, ensuring they have the support needed to reach their full potential. You install a drip irrigation system, and each morning, you enjoy the sight of water trickling down, nourishing every plant. You notice a few aphids and promptly spray them with a neem oil solution, ensuring your plants remain healthy and productive. This vertical garden becomes a vibrant tapestry of green, offering both visual delight and a bountiful harvest.

By incorporating vertical gardening solutions, you can transform even the smallest spaces into lush, productive gardens. This method not only maximizes growing space but also enhances the overall health and beauty of your garden. Vertical gardening offers a practical and innovative approach to growing a diverse range of plants, making it an excellent choice for urban and small-space gardeners.

8.4 CREATING MICROCLIMATES IN YOUR GARDEN

Understanding microclimates can significantly enhance your gardening success. A microclimate is a small area within your garden that has different temperature, moisture, or wind conditions compared to the overall environment. These variations can be influenced by factors like sunlight, wind, and moisture levels. For instance, a south-facing wall absorbs heat and creates a warmer microclimate, perfect for heat-loving plants. Conversely, a shaded area under a large tree might stay cooler and more humid, ideal for shade-tolerant species. Creating diverse microclimates allows you to grow a wider variety of plants by tailoring specific areas to their unique needs.

Identifying microclimates in your garden involves careful observation and monitoring. Begin by noting areas that receive varying amounts of sunlight throughout the day. Some spots might bask in full sun, while others remain in partial or full shade. Use a thermometer to check temperature differences in these areas at different times of the day. This will help you understand how much heat each spot retains or loses. Assess wind patterns by observing how wind moves through your garden. Note areas that are shielded by structures or trees and those exposed to strong gusts. Finally, monitor moisture levels by checking soil dampness regularly. Some areas might dry out quickly, while others retain moisture longer. These observations will help you map out the unique microclimates within your garden.

Creating and enhancing microclimates involves using various techniques to modify your garden's condition. Structures like walls, fences, and hedges serve as excellent windbreaks, reducing wind speed and creating sheltered areas. For instance, planting a row of dense shrubs along the edge of your garden can protect delicate plants from harsh winds. Installing shade cloths or pergolas can control sunlight exposure, providing shade for plants that need protection from intense sun. This is especially useful in hot climates where the midday sun can be too harsh. Raised beds and terraces improve drainage and can create slightly warmer microclimates due to the elevation. These are ideal for plants that require well-drained soil and slightly warmer conditions. Using mulch and ground covers helps retain soil moisture by reducing evaporation. Organic mulches like straw or wood chips not only conserve moisture but also improve soil structure as they decompose.

Microclimate Mapping Exercise

1. **Observe Sunlight:** Track sunlight exposure in different garden areas throughout the day.
2. **Measure Temperature:** Use a thermometer to record temperature variations in these areas.
3. **Assess Wind Patterns:** Note which areas are protected or exposed to wind.
4. **Check Moisture Levels:** Regularly monitor soil moisture in different spots.

Once you've mapped out your microclimates, you can strategically select and place plants based on these conditions. Choose plants that thrive in specific microclimates for optimal growth. For example, place sun-loving plants like tomatoes and peppers in the warm, sunny spots, while shade-tolerant plants like ferns and hostas can go in the cooler, shaded areas. Grouping plants with similar needs together makes it easier to manage their care. This approach ensures that each plant receives the right amount of light, water, and protection. Additionally, rotating crops to take advantage of seasonal microclimates can boost productivity. For instance, use cooler areas for spring and fall crops like lettuce and spinach, and reserve the warmer spots for summer crops like beans and cucumbers.

Understanding and utilizing microclimates in your garden allows you to create a more diverse and productive growing environment. By identifying existing microclimates, enhancing them through strategic modifications, and selecting plants suited to these conditions, you can optimize your garden's potential. This thoughtful approach not only maximizes your garden's productivity but also creates a more resilient and sustainable ecosystem.

In the next chapter, we will explore sustainable and eco-friendly practices, delving into techniques that not only benefit your garden but also contribute to the health of the environment.

CHAPTER 9
SUSTAINABLE AND ECO-FRIENDLY PRACTICES

This chapter will explore various water conservation methods that not only benefit your garden but also contribute to environmental sustainability.

9.1 WATER CONSERVATION METHODS

Rainwater harvesting is a practice that captures, diverts, and stores rainwater for garden use. It offers numerous benefits, including reducing reliance on municipal water, lowering water bills, and providing plants with pure, soft water that is near neutral pH. Installing rain barrels or cisterns is an effective way to collect rainwater from rooftops. Rain barrels can be placed under downspouts to capture runoff, and they come in various sizes to suit different needs. Cisterns, larger storage tanks, can hold significant amounts of water and are ideal for properties with substantial garden space. Using rain chains to direct water flow is both functional and aesthetically pleasing. These chains guide rainwater from gutters to storage containers or directly into garden beds, creating a soothing visual element. Implementing rain gardens is another excellent method to capture runoff. These gardens are designed to absorb and filter rainwater, reducing erosion and improving soil moisture. By strategically planting water-loving species in low-lying areas, you can create a beautiful and functional landscape feature.

Efficient irrigation systems are essential for water conservation in the garden. Drip irrigation systems deliver water directly to the plant roots, minimizing evaporation and runoff. These systems consist of a network of tubes and emitters that release water slowly and evenly. Drip irrigation is particularly beneficial for vegetable gardens and flower beds where precise watering is crucial. Soaker hoses are another effective option, providing even moisture distribution along their length. These hoses can be laid out around plant bases, and they release water gradually, ensuring deep soil penetration. Smart irrigation controllers take water efficiency to the next level by automating watering schedules based on weather conditions and soil moisture levels. These controllers adjust watering times and amounts, reducing water waste and ensuring optimal plant hydration.

Mulching is a simple yet powerful technique for conserving water in the garden. By covering the soil with a layer of organic or inorganic material, you can significantly reduce evaporation and maintain consistent soil moisture. Organic mulches, such as straw, wood chips, and compost, decompose over time, enriching the soil and improving its structure. Straw is excellent for vegetable gardens, while wood chips are ideal for perennial beds and around trees. Compost provides both moisture retention and nutrient benefits. Inorganic mulches, such as gravel and landscape fabric, also help conserve water and suppress weeds. Gravel is suitable for pathways and areas with succulents, while landscape fabric can be used under organic mulch to enhance its effectiveness. Proper mulching techniques involve spreading mulch evenly around plants, leaving a small gap around the stems to prevent rot. Replenish mulch layers as needed to maintain their effectiveness.

Selecting drought-tolerant plants is another crucial aspect of water conservation. These plants are adapted to thrive with minimal water, making them ideal for gardens in arid regions or during dry seasons. Native plants are particularly well-suited to local climate conditions and often require less water and maintenance. For example, in the southwestern United States, plants like lantana and coneflower are excellent choices. Succulents and xerophytic plants, which store water in their leaves, stems, or roots, are also great options. Varieties like agave and stonecrop can withstand prolonged periods without water. Mediterranean herbs, such as lavender and rosemary, are not only drought-tolerant but also add fragrance and beauty to the garden. These herbs thrive in well-drained soil and full sun, making them perfect for water-wise gardening.

To effectively implement water conservation methods, consider creating a water management plan for your garden. Assess your garden's water needs and identify areas where rainwater harvesting, efficient irrigation, mulching, and drought-tolerant plants can be integrated. By combining these strategies, you can create a resilient and sustainable garden that thrives even in challenging conditions. Remember, every drop of water saved contributes to a healthier environment and a more productive garden.

9.2 ORGANIC WEED MANAGEMENT

In the battle against weeds, prevention is your strongest ally. Preventive measures reduce the time and effort spent on weed control, allowing your plants to thrive without competition. One effective strategy is using landscape fabric or mulch to block light, which prevents weeds from germinating. Landscape fabric, when laid over the soil and covered with mulch, creates a physical barrier that stops weeds from emerging. Another approach is planting ground covers that outcompete weeds for sunlight and nutrients. Plants like clover, creeping thyme, or sweet woodruff spread quickly, forming a dense mat that suppresses weed growth. Implementing crop rotation also disrupts weed cycles by varying the types of plants grown in each area. This practice prevents weeds from becoming established and reduces the weed seed bank in the soil.

Mechanical weed control involves physically removing weeds without chemicals. Hand-pulling is a simple yet effective method, especially for small gardens or isolated weed patches. The key is to pull weeds when the soil is moist, ensuring the entire root system is removed to prevent regrowth. Using hoes and weeders can make the task more efficient, especially for larger areas. A sharp hoe can slice through weed stems just below the soil surface, cutting off their life source. Flame weeding, a less common but highly effective technique, uses a propane torch to burn weeds. The intense heat kills the plant tissues, causing the weeds to wither and die within days. It's especially useful for managing weeds in gravel paths, driveways, and other non-flammable areas.

Organic mulching is another powerful tool in your weed management arsenal. Applying a thick layer of organic mulch, such as straw, wood chips, or leaf litter, not only conserves soil moisture but also suppresses weeds by blocking light. Straw is particularly good for vegetable gardens, while wood chips work well around trees and shrubs. Leaf litter, when available, is an excellent free option that enriches the soil as it decomposes. Using cardboard or newspaper as a weed barrier under mulch can enhance its effectiveness. These materials decompose over time, adding organic matter to the soil. Maintaining mulch layers is crucial to keeping weeds at bay. Replenish mulch as it breaks down or becomes thin, ensuring a consistent barrier against weed growth.

Cover crops offer an organic method for weed suppression that also improves soil health. Selecting cover crops like clover, rye, or buckwheat can outcompete weeds for resources, reducing their presence in your garden. Clover, for instance, is a nitrogen-fixing plant that enriches the soil while providing ground cover. Rye and buckwheat grow quickly, shading out weeds and adding organic matter when turned into the soil. Timing the planting and termination of cover crops is essential for maximizing their weed-suppressing benefits. Plant cover crops in late summer or early fall, allowing them to establish before winter. In the spring, incorporate them into the soil as green manure, which adds nutrients and organic matter. This practice not only suppresses weeds but also enhances soil structure and fertility.

Incorporating these organic weed management strategies into your gardening routine creates a healthier, more productive environment for your plants. By focusing on prevention, mechanical control, organic mulching, and cover cropping, you can effectively manage weeds without resorting to chemicals. This holistic approach not only benefits your garden but also supports a more sustainable and eco-friendly way of growing.

9.3 CROP ROTATION AND SOIL HEALTH

Crop rotation is a practice that has been used for centuries to maintain soil health and increase crop yields. It involves changing the types of crops grown in each area of your garden from one season to the next. One of the fundamental principles of crop rotation is breaking pest and disease cycles. Different plants attract different pests and diseases. By rotating crops, you disrupt the life cycles of these pests and pathogens, reducing their chances of becoming established and causing harm. Additionally, rotating crops helps improve soil fertility and structure. Different plants have different nutrient needs and root structures. For example, legumes like beans and peas fix nitrogen in the soil, which benefits subsequent crops like corn that have high nitrogen demands. This natural replenishment of nutrients reduces the need for chemical fertilizers and promotes healthier soil.

Planning effective crop rotations requires a thoughtful approach, especially for different garden sizes. One method is to rotate plant families, such as legumes, brassicas (cabbage, broccoli), and nightshades (tomatoes, peppers). Each family has distinct nutrient needs and pest associations. By rotating these families, you balance nutrient use and minimize pest and disease risks. Creating multi-year rotation plans can further enhance the benefits. For example, you might plant legumes in one bed during the first year, followed by brassicas in the second year, and nightshades in the third year. This cycle ensures that no single nutrient is depleted, and pests do not become entrenched. Companion planting can also complement crop rotations. For instance, planting marigolds with tomatoes can deter nematodes and other pests, enhancing the overall health of your garden.

Cover crops and green manure play a vital role in crop rotation. These crops are grown primarily to improve soil health rather than for harvest. Selecting cover crops like clover, rye, or buckwheat can fix nitrogen, improve soil structure, and suppress weeds. Clover, for instance, is a nitrogen-fixing legume that enriches the soil, while rye and buckwheat grow quickly, providing ground cover that prevents erosion and suppresses weed growth. Timing the planting and incorporation of green manures is crucial. Plant cover crops in the off-season or after harvesting your main crops. Allow them to grow until just before they flower, then incorporate them into the soil. This process, known as green manuring, adds organic matter and nutrients to the soil, enhancing its fertility and structure.

Monitoring and adjusting crop rotations based on garden performance is essential for long-term success. Keeping detailed garden records helps track what was planted where and when. Note the health and yield of each crop, as well as any pest or disease issues. These records provide valuable insights into the effectiveness of your rotation plan. Observing plant health and soil conditions throughout the growing season allows you to make timely adjustments. For example, if you notice that a particular area of your garden consistently struggles with nutrient deficiencies or pest problems, consider altering the rotation plan for that section. Regular soil testing can also inform your decisions, helping you balance nutrient levels and adjust rotations as needed.

Crop rotation, combined with the use of cover crops and green manures, creates a sustainable and resilient gardening system. By rotating plant families, planning multi-year cycles, and incorporating green manures, you enhance soil health, balance nutrient use, and reduce pest and disease pressures. This holistic approach not only benefits your garden but also supports a more sustainable and eco-friendly way of growing.

9.4 BUILDING A POLLINATOR-FRIENDLY GARDEN

Pollinators are the unsung heroes of our gardens, playing an indispensable role in fruit and vegetable production. Bees, butterflies, and other pollinators transfer pollen from one flower to another, enabling fertilization and the growth of fruits and seeds. Without these diligent workers, many crops would fail to produce the bountiful harvests we rely on. Beyond their immediate impact on food production, pollinators contribute significantly to biodiversity. They support the growth of plants that provide food and habitats for other wildlife, creating a rich tapestry of life in our gardens. This interconnectedness underscores the importance of fostering a pollinator-friendly environment.

Selecting the right plants is crucial for attracting and supporting pollinators. Native plants are often the best choice as they have evolved alongside local pollinators, providing the nectar and pollen they need. Look for plants with high nectar and pollen content to ensure a steady food supply. Flowering herbs like lavender, thyme, and mint are excellent options. They not only attract pollinators but also add fragrance and culinary value to your garden. Incorporating a mix of perennials and annuals with staggered bloom times will ensure that there are always flowers available throughout the growing season. This continuous bloom cycle supports pollinators from early spring to late fall, providing them with the resources they need to thrive.

Creating habitats that support pollinator populations is another essential step. Installing bee hotels and nesting sites can provide much-needed shelter for solitary bees and other beneficial insects. These structures can be made from natural materials like bamboo, wood, and straw, and placed in sunny, sheltered spots. Providing water sources, such as shallow dishes filled with water and pebbles, gives pollinators a place to drink and cool off. Mud puddles can also be beneficial for butterflies, which extract essential minerals from the wet soil. To protect these delicate creatures, avoid using pesticides in your garden. Even organic pesticides can harm pollinators, so it's best to rely on natural pest control methods and encourage a balanced ecosystem that regulates pest populations naturally.

Sustainable gardening practices can greatly benefit pollinators and enhance your garden's overall health. Planting in clusters makes it easier for pollinators to find and feed on flowers, reducing the energy they expend searching for food. This approach also creates a more visually impactful garden design. Using organic pest control methods, such as introducing beneficial insects and using neem oil or insecticidal soap, helps maintain a healthy environment for pollinators. Ensuring a continuous bloom throughout the growing season is key. Plan your garden to include early, mid, and late-season bloomers, providing a steady food source. This not only supports pollinators but also keeps your garden vibrant and colorful all year round.

Building a pollinator-friendly garden is a rewarding endeavor that benefits both your plants and the broader ecosystem. By understanding the importance of pollinators, selecting the right plants, creating supportive habitats, and adopting sustainable practices, you can create a thriving garden that attracts and nurtures these vital creatures. The effort you put into fostering a pollinator-friendly environment will pay off in healthier plants, more abundant harvests, and a garden teeming with life.

As we close this chapter on sustainable and eco-friendly practices, remember that every small change you make in your garden can have a significant impact on the environment. Your efforts to conserve water, manage weeds organically, rotate crops, and support pollinators contribute to a more sustainable world. Next, we will delve into the practical aspects of harvesting and storing your garden's bounty, ensuring that you enjoy the fruits of your labor well beyond the growing season.

CHAPTER 10
HARVESTING AND STORAGE

This chapter will guide you through the art and science of harvesting, ensuring that you gather your fruits and vegetables at their absolute best.

10.1 HARVESTING TECHNIQUES FOR PEAK RIPENESS

Identifying peak ripeness involves keen observation and a bit of patience. Each type of produce has unique indicators signaling it's time to harvest. For instance, tomatoes turn fully red, signaling they're ready to be plucked. The color change is a clear sign that the sugars and acids have balanced, making the fruit sweet and tangy. Similarly, cucumbers should be firm to the touch, indicating they haven't become overripe and bitter. Bell peppers reach their peak when they have attained their full size and vibrant color, whether green, red, or yellow. Melons, on the other hand, emit a sweet fragrance when they are ripe, a subtle yet unmistakable cue that they are ready to be enjoyed.

The tools you use for harvesting can make a significant difference in the quality of your produce. Sharp knives or pruning shears are essential for harvesting fruits like tomatoes and peppers, as they ensure a clean cut that minimizes damage to both the fruit and the plant. For root vegetables like carrots and beets, a sturdy digging fork is invaluable. It allows you to lift the roots gently from the soil without breaking them. Delicate herbs, such as basil and parsley, are best harvested with scissors. Snipping them just above a leaf node encourages regrowth, ensuring a continuous supply of fresh herbs.

When it comes to the actual harvesting techniques, each type of produce requires a specific approach to avoid damage. For tomatoes, use a sharp knife or pruning shears to cut the stem, leaving a small portion attached to the fruit to prevent bruising. Peppers can be gently twisted off the plant, but make sure not to pull too hard to avoid damaging the plant. For root vegetables, insert a digging fork into the soil a few inches away from the plant and lift gently to loosen the soil before pulling the vegetable out by its base. Herbs should be snipped above a leaf node, which will encourage the plant to produce new growth, ensuring a continuous harvest.

Timing is everything when it comes to harvesting. The best time to harvest is in the early morning when the produce is cool and hydrated from the night. This is especially important for leafy greens, which can wilt quickly in the heat. Harvesting them early ensures they remain crisp and fresh. For crops like squash, wait until the skin is hard and unpierceable with a fingernail. This indicates they are fully mature and ready for storage. Leafy greens should be picked before they bolt, which is when they start to flower and become bitter. By paying attention to these subtle cues, you can ensure that your harvest is at its peak quality.

Harvesting Checklist

- Tomatoes: Fully red color, cut the stem with a knife.
- Cucumbers: Firm texture, pick before they become overripe.
- Bell Peppers: Full size and vibrant color, twist gently off the plant.
- Melons: Sweet fragrance, lift gently to check for ripeness.
- Root Vegetables: Use a digging fork, lift gently, pull by the base.
- Herbs: Snip above a leaf node, encourage regrowth.

Understanding these indicators and techniques will transform your harvesting experience. Not only will you ensure that your produce is at its peak, but you'll also preserve the health of your plants for future harvests. The joy of biting into a perfectly ripe tomato or savoring the sweetness of a freshly picked melon is unmatched. By mastering the art of harvesting, you bring the best flavors from your garden to your table.

10.2 STORING ROOT VEGETABLES

When it comes to extending the shelf life of root vegetables, proper preparation is key. After harvesting, begin by gently brushing off any excess soil without using water. Washing root vegetables before storage can introduce moisture, which promotes mold and rot. Instead, use a soft brush or cloth to remove dirt. Next, for crops like potatoes and sweet potatoes, curing is an important step. This process involves placing them in a warm, dry location for about 7 to 10 days. Curing helps to toughen their skins, which reduces moisture loss and extends their storage life. For vegetables like carrots and beets, it's crucial to remove the greens before storing them. Leaving the greens on can draw moisture away from the roots, causing them to shrivel. Simply snip off the greens about an inch above the root.

Storing root vegetables in the right conditions can make all the difference in how long they last. Most root vegetables thrive in cool, dark, and humid environments. A basement or a dedicated root cellar is ideal. Carrots and beets, for example, can be stored in containers filled with sand or sawdust. This method provides a humid environment that prevents them from drying out. Potatoes, on the other hand, should be stored in breathable containers, such as mesh bags or slatted crates, to prevent mold. The containers allow for airflow, which keeps the potatoes dry and reduces the risk of rot. Aim to keep the storage area between 32 and 40 degrees Fahrenheit with high humidity, around 90-95%. This combination of cool temperatures and humidity will maintain the freshness and firmness of your root vegetables.

Using a root cellar can be a game-changer for long-term storage. If you have one or plan to set one up, maintaining consistent temperature and humidity is essential. Root cellars naturally provide a cool and moist environment, but it's important to monitor these conditions regularly. Proper ventilation is also crucial to prevent mold and rot. Ensure that the cellar has vents or windows that can be opened to allow fresh air to circulate. When storing vegetables, layer them with straw or newspaper to create a buffer between layers and improve air circulation. This method also helps to absorb any excess moisture, further reducing the risk of spoilage.

Regularly checking on your stored vegetables is just as important as the initial preparation. Inspect them for signs of spoilage or mold, especially during the first few weeks of storage. Look for soft spots, discoloration, or a foul smell as indicators that something is wrong. Removing any rotting vegetables immediately is crucial to prevent the spread of mold to healthy ones. Additionally, practice rotating your stock, using the oldest produce first. This ensures that nothing goes to waste and that you're always consuming the freshest vegetables. By keeping a close eye on your stored vegetables, you can address issues early and maintain a supply of fresh produce throughout the off-season.

10.3 PRESERVING LEAFY GREENS

Preserving leafy greens requires a few essential steps to maintain their quality and nutritional value. Start by washing the greens thoroughly to remove any dirt or pests. After washing, dry them completely using a salad spinner or by patting them with a clean towel. Removing damaged or yellowed leaves is also important, as these can affect the quality of the preserved greens. Blanching is a critical step for preserving the vibrant color and nutrients of the greens. To blanch, bring a pot of water to a boil and immerse the greens for a brief period—two minutes for most greens and three minutes for tougher varieties like collards. Immediately transfer the greens to an ice water bath to stop the cooking process.

Freezing leafy greens is a straightforward way to preserve them. After blanching and cooling the greens, pat them dry to remove excess water. Spread the greens in a single layer on a baking tray and flash freeze them. Once frozen, transfer the greens to airtight freezer bags or containers. This method prevents the greens from clumping together, making it easier to use only what you need later. Freezing maintains the quality of the greens, ensuring they are ready to be used in soups, stews, and other dishes.

Dehydrating greens offers another long-term storage solution. Use a dehydrator or an oven set to a low temperature for this process. Arrange the greens in a single layer on the drying trays, ensuring they don't overlap. Dry the greens at 140°F for six to ten hours until they are crisp and brittle. Once dried, crumble the greens into a powder for easy use in soups and smoothies. Store the dried greens in airtight containers to keep out moisture and extend their shelf life.

Fermenting greens is an excellent method for adding a tangy flavor and preserving their nutritional benefits. Start by massaging the greens with salt to release their juices. Pack the greens tightly into jars, ensuring they are submerged in their brine. Allow the greens to ferment at room temperature for several days. The fermentation process not only preserves the greens but also enhances their probiotic content, contributing to gut health. Fermented greens can be used in salads, sandwiches, or as a side dish.

10.4 CANNING AND FREEZING FRUITS

Canning fruits is a traditional method that preserves them for long periods. Begin by sterilizing jars and lids to prevent contamination. Prepare the fruits by peeling, coring, and slicing them as needed. Using a water bath canner is suitable for high-acid fruits like berries and peaches. Place the prepared fruits in the jars, leaving some headspace, and fill with boiling water or syrup. Seal the jars and process them in the water bath canner to create a vacuum seal that preserves the fruit.

Freezing fruits is another effective way to retain their freshness and nutritional value. Wash, peel, and slice the fruits before laying them out on trays to flash freeze. This prevents the pieces from sticking together. Once frozen, transfer the fruit to airtight freezer bags, removing as much air as possible. This method preserves the texture and flavor of the fruits, making them ideal for baking, smoothies, or snacking.

Using frozen and canned fruits is versatile. Thaw frozen fruits for use in baking or smoothies. Canned fruits can be used in desserts, savory dishes, or made into sauces and compotes. The preserved fruits maintain their flavor and nutritional value, allowing you to enjoy the taste of summer year-round.

10.5 PRESERVING LEAFY GREENS

Preserving leafy greens starts with meticulous preparation. Begin by washing your greens thoroughly to remove any dirt or pests. Use cool running water and gently swish the leaves around in a large basin. Once washed, drying them is crucial to prevent excess moisture, which can lead to spoilage. A salad spinner works wonders here, but if you don't have one, pat the leaves dry with a clean towel. Next, inspect the greens and remove any damaged or yellowing leaves. These can affect the quality of your preserved greens. Blanching is the next key step to preserving color and nutrients. Bring a large pot of water to a rolling boil and prepare an ice water bath on the side. Submerge the greens in the boiling water for about two minutes, then quickly transfer them to the ice water bath to stop the cooking process. This not only locks in vibrant color but also helps retain essential nutrients.

Freezing leafy greens is a straightforward and effective method to maintain their quality. After blanching and shocking the greens in ice water, ensure they are thoroughly dry by patting them down with a towel. Spread the blanched greens in a single layer on a baking tray to flash freeze them. This prevents the leaves from sticking together. Once frozen, transfer the greens into airtight freezer bags or containers. Ensure you remove as much air as possible from the bags to prevent freezer burn. Label the bags with the date and type of greens, so you can easily keep track of what you have. This method ensures that you have a supply of fresh-tasting greens ready to be used in soups, stews, and other dishes throughout the year.

Dehydrating leafy greens offers another long-term storage option. Using a dehydrator or an oven set to a low temperature, arrange the greens in a single layer on the drying trays. Make sure the leaves do not overlap to ensure even drying. Set the dehydrator or oven to 140°F and dry the greens for about six to ten hours, until they become crisp and brittle. Once dried, you can crumble the greens into a fine powder, which is perfect for adding to soups, smoothies, and sauces. Store the dried greens in airtight containers to keep out moisture. This method not only preserves the greens for long periods but also concentrates their flavors and nutrients.

Fermenting leafy greens is a wonderful way to preserve them while adding a unique tangy flavor. Start by massaging the greens with salt to release their juices. Use about one tablespoon of salt per quart of greens. The salt helps to draw out the moisture, creating a natural brine. Once the greens are sufficiently massaged and have released enough liquid, pack them tightly into sterilized jars. Press down firmly to ensure the greens are submerged in their own juices. If necessary, add a bit of water to cover the greens completely. Seal the jars and leave them at room temperature for several days to ferment. The process of fermentation not only preserves the greens but also enhances their probiotic content, making them beneficial for gut health. After the initial fermentation period, store the jars in the refrigerator to slow down the fermentation process and keep the greens fresh.

Preserving leafy greens through these methods ensures that you have a steady supply of nutritious and flavorful greens year-round. Whether you choose to freeze, dehydrate, or ferment, each technique offers unique benefits and preserves the quality of the greens. With a bit of preparation and the right techniques, you can enjoy the taste and nutrition of fresh greens long after the growing season has ended.

10.6 CANNING AND FREEZING FRUITS

Canning fruits is a time-honored method that allows you to savor the flavors of summer long after the harvest season has ended. The process begins with sterilizing jars and lids to ensure they are free from any bacteria that could spoil the fruit. To do this, boil the jars and lids in water for at least ten minutes. Once sterilized, it's time to prepare the fruits. This involves peeling, coring, and slicing them as needed. For high-acid fruits like strawberries, peaches, and apples, a water bath canner is the preferred method. Place the prepared fruits in the jars, leaving some headspace, and fill the jars with boiling water or syrup. Seal the jars properly to create a vacuum, which will preserve the fruit by keeping out air and bacteria. The sealed jars are then processed in the water bath canner according to the fruit's specific time requirements, ensuring they are safely preserved for long-term storage.

For those who seek to add a touch of culinary delight to their pantry, specific canning recipes can elevate the experience. Strawberry jam is a classic favorite. Begin by mashing fresh strawberries and combining them with sugar and lemon juice. Cook the mixture until it reaches the desired thickness, then ladle it into sterilized jars. Process the jars in a water bath canner for about ten minutes. Peach preserves follow a similar process but involve peeling and slicing the peaches before cooking them with sugar and lemon juice. Apple butter requires a bit more time, as you need to cook apples with spices like cinnamon and nutmeg until they are soft, then blend them into a smooth consistency. The mixture is then cooked further until thickened and processed in jars for long-term enjoyment.

Freezing fruits is another excellent way to preserve their freshness and nutritional value. Start by washing the fruits thoroughly. For fruits like peaches and apples, peeling and slicing are necessary steps. Once prepared, arrange the fruit slices in a single layer on baking trays and flash freeze them. This step prevents the pieces from clumping together. After the fruit is frozen solid, transfer them to airtight freezer bags, making sure to remove as much air as possible to prevent freezer burn. Label the bags with the date and type of fruit for easy identification. This method ensures that the fruits retain their texture and flavor, making them perfect for future use in various recipes.

Using frozen and canned fruits adds versatility to your culinary repertoire. Thaw frozen fruits for baking, where they can bring a burst of flavor to pies, muffins, and cakes. They are also perfect for smoothies, adding a touch of summer sweetness even in the depths of winter. Canned fruits, on the other hand, can be used in a variety of dishes, both sweet and savory. They make excellent additions to desserts like cobblers and crisps. You can also incorporate them into savory recipes, such as using canned peaches or apricots in a glaze for roasted meats. Additionally, making fruit sauces and compotes from preserved fruits is a delightful way to use them. Simply simmer the canned fruits with a bit of sugar and spices until they reach the desired consistency. These sauces can then be drizzled over pancakes, waffles, or ice cream, adding a touch of homemade goodness to any meal.

Preserving fruits through canning and freezing allows you to enjoy the bounty of your garden throughout the year. By mastering these techniques, you ensure that the flavors of your harvest remain vibrant and accessible, enhancing your meals and providing a taste of summer even in the coldest months. As we look ahead to the next chapter, we'll explore troubleshooting and problem-solving in the garden, helping you address common issues and maintain a thriving, productive space.

CHAPTER 11
TROUBLESHOOTING AND PROBLEM SOLVING

Plants, like us, require a balanced diet. When they don't get the nutrients they need, they show it in various ways. Understanding these signals can be the difference between a lush garden and one that struggles.

11.1 DIAGNOSING NUTRIENT DEFICIENCIES

Plants rely on various nutrients to grow, thrive, and produce healthy yields. These nutrients fall into three main categories: macronutrients, secondary nutrients, and micronutrients. Macronutrients are required in larger amounts and include nitrogen, phosphorus, and potassium. Nitrogen is essential for leafy growth and overall plant vigor. It plays a critical role in photosynthesis and the production of chlorophyll. Phosphorus is vital for root development and energy transfer within the plant. It supports the formation of flowers and fruits. Potassium aids in water regulation, disease resistance, and overall plant health. It helps plants withstand stress and improves the quality of fruits and vegetables.

Secondary nutrients, needed in moderate amounts, include calcium, magnesium, and sulfur. Calcium strengthens cell walls, promoting sturdy growth and preventing disorders like blossom end rot in tomatoes. Magnesium is a key component of chlorophyll, essential for photosynthesis. It also aids in enzyme activation and nutrient uptake. Sulfur is crucial for protein synthesis and the formation of certain vitamins. It supports overall plant metabolism and growth. Micronutrients, required in trace amounts, include iron, manganese, and zinc. Iron is critical for chlorophyll synthesis and oxygen transport within the plant. Manganese plays a role in photosynthesis, respiration, and nitrogen assimilation. Zinc is essential for enzyme function, protein synthesis, and growth regulation. While plants need these nutrients in smaller quantities, their absence can lead to significant deficiencies and hinder overall plant health.

Identifying nutrient deficiencies involves keen observation of your plants. Common symptoms can help you diagnose and address these issues promptly. Yellowing leaves, or chlorosis, often indicate a nitrogen deficiency. This condition affects older leaves first, as nitrogen is mobile within the plant and moves to new growth. Purple or reddish leaves suggest a phosphorus deficiency. This symptom is more noticeable on older leaves and can also result in stunted growth and poor root development. Brown leaf edges, also known as leaf scorch, are a sign of potassium deficiency. Potassium is crucial for water regulation, and its absence leads to water stress symptoms. Interveinal chlorosis, where the areas between leaf veins turn yellow while the veins remain green, signals a magnesium deficiency. This condition typically affects older leaves and can lead to reduced photosynthesis and poor growth.

To accurately diagnose nutrient deficiencies, soil testing is essential. Start by collecting soil samples from various areas of your garden. Use a clean trowel to dig small holes, about 6 inches deep, and take a sample from each spot. Combine these samples in a clean container, mix them thoroughly, and air-dry them if needed. Soil test kits, available at garden centers, allow you to test for pH and nutrient levels at home. Alternatively, you can send samples to a laboratory for a comprehensive analysis. Follow the kit or lab instructions for accurate results. Interpreting soil test results can be straightforward; most reports provide recommendations based on your garden's needs. Understanding these results helps you make informed decisions about soil amendments and fertilizers.

Correcting nutrient deficiencies involves adding the right amendments to your soil. For nitrogen deficiencies, incorporate compost or organic fertilizers like blood meal or fish emulsion. These amendments provide a slow-release source of nitrogen, improving soil fertility over time. Phosphorus deficiencies can be addressed with bone meal or rock phosphate. These amendments are rich in phosphorus and help strengthen root development and flower production. To correct potassium deficiencies, apply wood ash or kelp meal. These natural sources of potassium enhance water regulation and overall plant health. For magnesium deficiencies, incorporate Epsom salts into your soil. Epsom salts, made of magnesium sulfate, are easily absorbed by plants and help restore healthy green foliage.

Nutrient Deficiency Checklist

1. **Observe Symptoms**: Identify yellowing leaves, purple or reddish leaves, brown leaf edges, and interveinal chlorosis.
2. **Collect Soil Samples**: Gather samples from different garden areas.
3. **Test Soil**: Use soil test kits or send samples to a lab.
4. **Interpret Results**: Understand nutrient levels and deficiencies.
5. **Add Amendments**: Use compost for nitrogen, bone meal for phosphorus, wood ash for potassium, and Epsom salts for magnesium.
6. **Monitor Plant Health**: Regularly check for improvement and adjust as needed.

Understanding and addressing nutrient deficiencies ensures your plants receive the balanced diet they need to thrive. By observing symptoms, testing your soil, and applying the correct amendments, you can maintain a healthy, productive garden.

11.2 DEALING WITH DROUGHT STRESS

Wilting or drooping leaves are the first indicators that a plant is struggling to access enough water. Leaf curl and browning edges follow, a plant's desperate attempt to conserve moisture. Stunted growth and reduced flowering are more subtle signs but equally telling. These symptoms indicate that the plant is diverting its limited resources to survival rather than growth. Premature leaf drop is another distress signal, a plant's way of reducing its water needs by shedding leaves.

To help your plants cope with drought, effective watering strategies are crucial. Deep watering is one of the most effective methods. Instead of frequent, shallow watering, focus on deep watering to encourage roots to grow deeper into the soil. This makes plants more resilient during droughts. Using drip irrigation is another excellent strategy. It targets water directly to the root zones, reducing evaporation and ensuring that water reaches where it's needed most. Watering early in the morning is also beneficial. The temperatures are cooler, reducing evaporation and allowing plants to absorb water before the heat of the day sets in.

Improving soil's water retention capacity can significantly mitigate drought stress. Adding organic matter like compost or well-rotted manure is one of the best ways to enhance soil structure and water-holding capacity. These materials improve the soil's ability to retain moisture, reducing the frequency of watering needed. Water-absorbing crystals or hydrogels are another option. These substances absorb water and slowly release it into the soil, providing a steady moisture supply to plants. Mulching is also incredibly effective. A thick layer of mulch reduces evaporation from the soil surface, maintains soil moisture, and keeps roots cool. Organic mulches like straw, wood chips, or leaves break down over time, adding valuable organic matter to the soil.

Selecting and planting drought-tolerant species is a proactive way to manage drought stress. Native plants are often the best choice, as they are adapted to local conditions and require less water and maintenance. For vegetables, consider drought-resistant varieties like okra and eggplant. These crops are naturally more resilient to dry conditions and can still produce a bountiful harvest with minimal water. Incorporating succulents and other xerophytic plants into your garden can also be beneficial. These plants are specifically adapted to survive in arid conditions, storing water in their leaves, stems, or roots. They add variety and beauty to your garden while being highly efficient in water use.

Drought Stress Management Checklist

1. **Recognize Symptoms**: Look for wilting leaves, leaf curl, browning edges, stunted growth, and premature leaf drop.
2. **Deep Watering**: Water deeply to encourage deep root growth.
3. **Drip Irrigation**: Use drip systems to target root zones.
4. **Morning Watering**: Water early in the morning to reduce evaporation.
5. **Add Organic Matter**: Incorporate compost or well-rotted manure to improve soil water retention.
6. **Use Hydrogels**: Apply water-absorbing crystals to maintain steady moisture.
7. **Mulch**: Spread a thick layer of mulch to reduce evaporation and maintain soil moisture.
8. **Choose Drought-Tolerant Plants**: Select native plants, drought-resistant vegetables like okra and eggplant, and succulents.

By observing these strategies, you can help your garden withstand drought conditions more effectively. Your plants will be healthier, more resilient, and better able to cope with the challenges of a dry climate.

11.3 ADDRESSING OVERWATERING PROBLEMS

Overwatering can be just as harmful as drought. Recognizing the signs early can save your plants. Yellowing leaves and soft stems are often the first indicators, as excess water drowns roots, preventing them from absorbing oxygen. This leads to a lack of essential nutrients reaching the foliage. Root rot and fungal growth are more severe consequences. You might notice a foul smell emanating from the soil, indicating decaying roots. Plants may also wilt despite the soil being wet, a paradox that confuses many gardeners. Additionally, algae or moss growth on the soil surface is a clear sign that the ground remains too wet for too long.

Improving soil drainage is crucial to preventing these issues. If you have heavy clay soil, consider adding sand or perlite. These materials help break up the dense structure, allowing water to flow more freely and air to penetrate to the roots. Creating raised beds or mounds is another effective strategy. Elevated soil levels naturally drain better, reducing the risk of waterlogging. For more persistent drainage problems, installing drainage systems like French drains can be a game-changer. These involve creating a trench filled with gravel and a perforated pipe, redirecting water away from your garden beds.

Adjusting your watering practices can also make a significant difference. Instead of frequent, shallow watering, aim to water less often but more deeply. This encourages roots to grow deeper into the soil, making plants more resilient and less susceptible to surface water issues. Allowing the soil to dry out between waterings is crucial. It helps prevent the buildup of excess moisture around the roots. Using a moisture meter can be incredibly helpful in this regard. These devices provide real-time data on soil moisture levels, ensuring you only water when necessary.

Addressing root rot caused by overwatering requires prompt action. Start by removing the affected plants from the soil. Trim away any diseased or decayed roots with sterilized pruning shears.

Once you've pruned the unhealthy parts, replant the affected plants in well-draining soil. It's essential to reduce the frequency of watering during the recovery period. This helps the plant re-establish its root system without the risk of further rot. In severe cases, applying fungicides may be necessary to combat fungal infections in the soil. Always follow the manufacturer's instructions and consider using organic options whenever possible.

Overwatering can be a silent killer in the garden. By recognizing the symptoms early, improving drainage, adjusting watering practices, and addressing root rot, you can prevent it from wreaking havoc on your plants. These steps not only save your current garden but also build a more resilient and thriving environment for future growth.

11.4 MANAGING POOR SOIL DRAINAGE

Recognizing poor soil drainage is crucial for maintaining healthy plants. One of the first signs is water pooling on the soil surface during and after rain or irrigation. This stagnation indicates that the soil is not allowing water to infiltrate quickly enough. Slow water infiltration is another indicator. When water takes too long to soak into the ground, it means the soil's structure is compacted or filled with fine particles that impede drainage. Plants suffering from root rot or yellowing leaves often signal underlying drainage issues. These symptoms occur because excess water drowns the roots, depriving them of oxygen and leading to decay.

Improving soil drainage starts with the right amendments. Adding coarse sand or grit to heavy clay soils can significantly enhance drainage. The larger particles create spaces in the soil, allowing water to move through more freely. Another effective amendment is incorporating organic matter like compost or leaf mold. These materials improve soil structure by increasing its porosity, which helps water penetrate more efficiently. Gypsum is particularly useful for breaking up compacted clay soils. It works by displacing sodium ions that cause clay particles to bind tightly together, making the soil more friable and improving its drainage capacity.

Creating raised beds is another practical solution for poor soil drainage. Raised beds elevate the soil above the natural ground level, which helps with water runoff and air circulation around the roots. When building raised beds, use a well-draining soil mix composed of equal parts topsoil, compost, and coarse sand or perlite. This mix ensures that water moves through the soil instead of pooling at the surface. The height and width of the beds are also important. A height of 12 to 18 inches is usually sufficient to improve drainage, while a width of 3 to 4 feet allows easy access and maintenance. You can construct raised beds using various materials such as wood, stone, or metal. Wood is a popular choice because it's easy to work with and relatively inexpensive. Stone and metal beds are more durable and add an aesthetic appeal to the garden.

For severe drainage problems, installing drainage systems can be highly effective. French drains are a common solution. Constructing a French drain involves digging a trench, filling it with gravel, and laying a perforated pipe at the bottom. The trench is then covered with more gravel and soil. This setup redirects excess water away from garden beds, preventing waterlogging. Installing perforated pipes or drainage tiles is another method. These pipes allow water to escape from the soil and flow away, reducing the risk of root rot. Creating swales or berms can also manage water flow effectively. Swales are shallow ditches that capture and redirect water, while berms are raised areas that help control water movement and prevent erosion.

By addressing poor soil drainage with these practical solutions, you can ensure that your plants thrive in a healthy environment. Recognizing the signs of poor drainage, using the right amendments, creating raised beds, and installing effective drainage systems will transform your garden into a more resilient and productive space. In the next chapter, we will explore the final steps in maintaining a healthy garden, focusing on seasonal care and advanced techniques.

CHAPTER 12
INSPIRATIONAL CASE STUDIES AND RESOURCES

This chapter is dedicated to sharing some of these inspirational tales, showcasing the power of gardening to change lives and spaces.

12.1 SUCCESS STORIES FROM HOME GARDENERS

From Lawn to Garden: A Family's Green Journey

Transforming a suburban lawn into a productive vegetable garden is no small feat, but one family in the Midwest did just that. Their front yard, once a neatly trimmed expanse of grass, is now a thriving vegetable garden. Rows of tomatoes, peppers, and beans replace the monotony of a green lawn. Their journey began with a desire to grow their own food and reduce their environmental footprint. They started small, converting a section of their lawn into garden beds. Over the years, they expanded, adding compost bins and rain barrels to manage waste and water efficiently. Today, their garden not only feeds their family but also serves as an educational space for neighbors curious about organic gardening.

Small Space, Big Harvest: Balcony Gardening Success

In an urban setting, space is often a limiting factor, but one resourceful gardener turned a small balcony into a lush oasis. Using container gardening, they cultivated a variety of vegetables, from leafy greens to cherry tomatoes. Vertical gardening techniques, with trellises and hanging pots, maximized the limited space. The balcony, once cluttered with unused items, became a vibrant, productive garden. This transformation was more than aesthetic; it provided a source of fresh, organic produce and a relaxing green space amidst the city's hustle. The gardener's innovative use of space inspired other apartment dwellers to start their own container gardens, proving that you don't need a large yard to enjoy the benefits of gardening.

Retirement Renaissance: Backyard Transformed Into Oasis

Retirement often brings a desire to reconnect with nature, and for one retiree, it meant transforming a neglected backyard into a lush fruit and vegetable oasis. The yard, overgrown with weeds and debris, was cleared and rejuvenated with rich compost and organic soil amendments. Raised beds were built to grow a variety of fruits and vegetables. The retiree meticulously planned the garden layout, ensuring optimal sunlight and water access for each plant. Over time, the garden flourished, producing bountiful harvests of strawberries, lettuce, and zucchini. The transformation was not just physical; it brought a sense of purpose and joy, turning daily gardening tasks into meditative routines.

Soil Revival: Turning Barren Yard Into Fertile Garden

Overcoming challenges is a common theme in gardening, and one gardener faced the daunting task of improving poor soil conditions. The soil in their yard was compacted and nutrient-poor, making it difficult for plants to thrive. Through diligent composting and the addition of organic soil amendments like worm castings and aged manure, the soil gradually improved. Raised beds were constructed to further enhance soil quality and drainage. Today, the once barren yard is a fertile garden, teeming with healthy plants and vibrant flowers. The gardener's perseverance paid off, showing that with patience and the right techniques, even the most challenging soil can be transformed.

Drought-Proof Gardening: Water Conservation in Action

In a drought-prone area, water scarcity can be a significant hurdle. One innovative gardener implemented a range of water-saving techniques to maintain a healthy garden. Drip irrigation systems were installed to deliver water directly to the plant roots, minimizing evaporation. Mulching with organic materials like straw and wood chips helped retain soil moisture. The gardener also collected rainwater in barrels to supplement their watering needs. These efforts not only conserved water but also created a sustainable garden that thrived despite the harsh conditions. The success of this garden inspired others in the community to adopt similar water-saving practices.

Aphid Battle: Organic Pest Control Victory

Managing pest infestations organically can be a challenging but rewarding endeavor. One gardener faced a severe aphid infestation that threatened their vegetable garden. Instead of resorting to chemical pesticides, they introduced beneficial insects like ladybugs and lacewings, which naturally prey on aphids. Companion planting strategies were also employed, with plants like marigolds and nasturtiums acting as natural pest repellents. These organic methods effectively controlled the pest population, leading to a bountiful harvest. The gardener's experience demonstrated that with knowledge and perseverance, organic pest control can be both effective and environmentally friendly.

Vertical Gardening: Maximizing Space and Productivity

Innovative techniques can maximize gardening efforts, especially in limited spaces. One gardener utilized vertical gardening to grow more in a small backyard. Trellises, wall planters, and vertical towers allowed them to cultivate a variety of vegetables and flowers without taking up much ground space. This method not only increased the garden's productivity but also enhanced its aesthetic appeal. Another gardener embraced permaculture principles, creating a self-sustaining garden that mimicked natural ecosystems. By integrating diverse plant species and using natural resources efficiently, they developed a garden that required minimal maintenance while providing abundant yields.

Year-Round Harvest: Extending the Growing Season

Creating a year-round garden is a dream for many, and one gardener achieved this using season extension techniques like hoop houses and cold frames. These structures protected plants from frost and extended the growing season by several months. The gardener could harvest fresh vegetables even in the colder months, reducing their reliance on store-bought produce. These innovative techniques allowed them to enjoy homegrown food year-round, showcasing the possibilities of gardening beyond the traditional growing season.

Family Bonds: Gardening Together

Gardening's impact extends beyond the physical transformation of spaces; it fosters personal growth and community connections. One family found that gardening together strengthened their bonds. Planting seeds, tending to plants, and harvesting produce became shared activities that brought them closer. Their garden became a place of learning and bonding, fostering a sense of togetherness.

Community Bloom: Inspiring Organic Gardens Across the Neighborhood

Another gardener's success inspired neighbors to start their own organic gardens. Seeing the lush, productive garden next door motivated others to try their hand at gardening, creating a ripple effect of green spaces throughout the neighborhood. The gardener's willingness to share knowledge and seedlings helped build a supportive gardening community.

Gardening Generosity: From Home Garden to Food Bank

In some cases, surplus produce from home gardens has contributed to local food security. One gardener regularly donated excess vegetables to a nearby food bank, providing fresh, organic produce to those in need. This act of generosity not only helped address food scarcity but also highlighted the potential of home gardens to support community well-being.

These success stories illustrate the profound impact of gardening on individuals and communities. Whether transforming a suburban lawn, overcoming soil challenges, or using innovative techniques, these gardeners have shown that dedication, creativity, and a love for nature can lead to remarkable transformations.

12.2 COMMUNITY GARDENING PROJECTS

Benefits of Community Gardens

Community gardening projects offer a multitude of benefits for both individuals and the larger community. One of the most immediate advantages is providing access to fresh, organic produce for urban residents. In many cities, fresh fruits and vegetables are not easily accessible, and community gardens help bridge this gap. By growing their own food, participants gain direct control over what they eat, ensuring it's free from harmful pesticides and chemicals.

Beyond the tangible benefits of fresh produce, community gardens foster a sense of community and cooperation. Working alongside neighbors to plant, tend, and harvest a garden builds strong social bonds. It creates a shared space where people from different backgrounds can come together, share their gardening knowledge, and support each other. This sense of community is often accompanied by a heightened sense of responsibility and pride in the garden's success, fostering a cooperative spirit that extends beyond the garden itself.

Community gardens also serve as educational hubs, offering numerous opportunities for skill-building and learning. From teaching children the basics of gardening and nutrition to providing adults with workshops on composting and sustainable practices, these gardens become centers of knowledge. Schools often integrate community gardens into their curriculum, giving students hands-on experience with planting, nurturing, and harvesting crops. This hands-on learning not only imparts practical skills but also instills a deeper appreciation for nature and the environment.

Case Studies of Successful Projects

Vacant to Vibrant: A City-Led Community Garden Revival

One inspiring example of a successful community gardening project is a city-led initiative that transformed vacant lots into thriving community gardens. These neglected spaces, once eyesores in the neighborhood, were revitalized with the help of local residents and city officials. The community came together to clean up the lots, build raised beds, and plant a variety of fruits, vegetables, and flowers. The transformation was remarkable, turning blighted areas into vibrant green spaces that now provide fresh produce and a gathering place for the community.

Growing Minds: School Gardens for Education and Nutrition

Another impactful project is a school garden program that teaches children about organic gardening and nutrition. In partnership with local schools, this program integrates gardening into the curriculum, allowing students to learn about plant biology, soil health, and sustainable practices. The garden serves as an outdoor classroom where students can engage in hands-on activities, from planting seeds to harvesting vegetables. This experience not only enhances their understanding of science and the environment but also encourages healthy eating habits.

Cultivating Connections: A Neighborhood Garden for Unity and Sustainability

A neighborhood garden project that promotes social cohesion and environmental stewardship has also seen great success. Residents collaborated to create a community garden in a shared space, planting a diverse array of crops and flowers. The project included educational workshops on composting, water conservation, and organic pest control. The garden became a focal point for community events, bringing people together for harvest festivals, gardening workshops, and communal meals. This project not only beautified the neighborhood but also fostered a strong sense of community and environmental awareness.

Starting a Community Garden

Starting a community garden begins with securing a suitable location and obtaining the necessary permissions. Look for vacant lots, unused schoolyards, or other open spaces that could be transformed into a garden. Contact local government agencies or property owners to get the required approvals. Once you have a location, the next step is organizing volunteers and establishing a governance structure. Form a committee to oversee the project, delegate tasks, and ensure smooth operation.

Sourcing funding and materials is crucial for the garden's success. Apply for grants from local governments, environmental organizations, or community foundations. Seek donations of seeds, tools, and building materials from local businesses and community members. Crowdfunding campaigns can also be effective in raising funds and engaging the broader community.

Planning and designing the garden layout based on community needs is the next step. Consider the types of plants that will be grown, the layout of garden beds, and the placement of pathways and communal areas. Involve community members in the planning process to ensure the garden meets their needs and preferences. Create a detailed plan that includes a timeline, budget, and list of necessary materials.

Maintaining and Growing the Project

Maintaining and growing a community garden requires ongoing effort and engagement. Establish regular workdays and maintenance schedules to ensure the garden is well-tended. Rotate tasks among volunteers to distribute the workload evenly. Hosting workshops and events can keep the community engaged and educated. Offer classes on topics like composting, organic pest control, and seasonal planting. These events not only provide valuable knowledge but also foster a sense of ownership and pride in the garden.

Creating partnerships with local businesses, schools, and organizations can provide additional support and resources. Collaborate with local nurseries for plant donations, schools for educational programs, and environmental groups for expertise and funding. Documenting and sharing the project's progress and successes is essential for attracting more support. Use social media, newsletters, and community bulletin boards to keep everyone informed and involved. Share stories of the garden's impact, from increased access to fresh produce to strengthened community bonds. This transparency and communication can help sustain and expand the project over time.

12.3 ONLINE RESOURCES AND GARDENING COMMUNITIES

In today's digital age, the wealth of information available online can greatly enhance your gardening experience. Educational websites and blogs are invaluable resources for organic gardeners. Websites like "Joe Gardener" and "Mother Earth News" provide comprehensive gardening guides and tutorials, covering everything from soil preparation to pest management. These platforms offer step-by-step instructions and practical tips, making complex gardening concepts accessible. Blogs such as "Gardenerd" and "Tending My Garden" share personal experiences, tips, and advice from seasoned gardeners. These narratives offer a relatable perspective, often highlighting the trials and triumphs of organic gardening. Additionally, online databases for plant varieties and growing conditions, like the USDA Plant Hardiness Zone Map, can help you choose the right plants for your specific climate and soil conditions.

Gardening forums and discussion groups are another excellent way to seek advice and share experiences with fellow gardeners. Forums dedicated to organic gardening techniques and practices, such as "The Organic Gardener" on Reddit, provide a space for gardeners to ask questions, share tips, and discuss challenges. These platforms are a goldmine of information, with experienced gardeners often offering solutions to common problems. Discussion groups focusing on specific gardening challenges, like pest management or soil health, allow you to dive deeper into particular topics. Sharing photos and progress updates on platforms like "GardenWeb" fosters a sense of community and allows for visual learning. Seeing other gardeners' successes and learning from their mistakes can be incredibly motivating and educational.

Social media has become a vibrant hub for gardening communities. Facebook groups focused on organic gardening and sustainable practices, such as "Organic Gardening for Beginners," are great for connecting with like-minded individuals. These groups often feature posts on garden updates, tips, and Q&A sessions. Instagram accounts like "@urbanorganicgardener" showcase inspiring garden transformations and tips, providing a visual feast of beautifully cultivated gardens. YouTube channels, such as "Epic Gardening," offer instructional videos on various gardening topics, from seed starting to composting. These videos are especially useful for visual learners who benefit from seeing techniques in action. Reddit communities like "r/gardening" are also popular for exchanging knowledge and experiences, with threads covering a wide range of gardening topics.

Gardening apps and digital tools can simplify many aspects of garden management. Apps like "Gardenize" and "From Seed to Spoon" help you track planting schedules, garden tasks, and weather conditions. These tools provide reminders for watering, fertilizing, and harvesting, ensuring that no task is overlooked. Plant identification apps like "PlantSnap" and "PictureThis" are incredibly useful for identifying plants and diagnosing issues. Simply take a photo, and the app provides detailed information about the plant and any potential problems. Weather and climate apps tailored to gardening needs, such as "My Garden Weather," offer forecasts and alerts specific to your garden's location. This helps you plan activities and protect your plants from adverse weather conditions.

Online resources and gardening communities offer a treasure trove of knowledge, support, and inspiration. Whether you prefer reading detailed guides, participating in forums, or watching instructional videos, there is something for every type of learner. Engaging with these resources can enhance your gardening skills, provide solutions to challenges, and connect you with a broader community of passionate gardeners. So, explore these digital tools and communities to enrich your gardening experience and grow your garden knowledge.

12.4 CONTINUING EDUCATION AND ADVANCED COURSES

Participating in local extension programs can be a game-changer for anyone looking to deepen their gardening knowledge. Local agricultural extension services often offer workshops that provide hands-on learning experiences. These workshops cover a range of topics, from soil health and composting to pest management and advanced planting techniques. They are usually led by experts who bring years of experience and practical insights, making complex topics easier to understand.

Another invaluable resource is the Master Gardener programs offered by many extension services. These programs provide in-depth training on various aspects of gardening, including plant biology, soil science, and sustainable practices. Becoming a Master Gardener not only equips you with advanced skills but also connects you with a network of like-minded individuals. You get the chance to volunteer and share your knowledge with the community, making a positive impact while continuing your learning journey.

Field days and demonstration gardens are another excellent way to learn best practices. These events showcase real-world applications of gardening techniques, allowing you to see firsthand how different methods work. You can walk through demonstration gardens, observe the results of various soil amendments, and ask questions directly to the experts. These experiences provide practical insights that you can apply to your own garden.

Online courses and webinars offer a flexible way to continue your gardening education. MOOCs (Massive Open Online Courses) on platforms like Coursera and edX cover topics such as organic gardening and sustainable agriculture. These courses are often created by universities and provide a comprehensive curriculum that you can follow at your own pace. Webinars hosted by gardening experts and organizations offer the latest insights and tips. They often include Q&A sessions, allowing you to get personalized advice on your gardening challenges.

For those looking to gain formal recognition, online certificate programs in horticulture and permaculture are a great option. These programs offer structured learning paths and often include practical assignments. Completing a certificate program not only enhances your skills but also adds credibility to your gardening expertise. Programs like those offered by the University of California and the Permaculture Institute are well-regarded and provide in-depth knowledge on advanced gardening topics.

Gardening books and publications are timeless resources that can enrich your understanding of organic gardening. Classic texts such as "The Vegetable Gardener's Bible" by Edward C. Smith and "The Organic Gardener's Handbook of Natural Pest and Disease Control" provide foundational knowledge and practical tips. Specialty books like "Teaming with Microbes" delve into advanced topics like soil science, offering insights into the complex world of soil organisms and their role in plant health. Gardening magazines such as "Mother Earth News" and "Organic Gardening" offer seasonal tips, the latest trends, and inspiring stories from gardeners around the world.

Professional associations and conferences are excellent for networking and continued education. Joining associations like the American Horticultural Society or the Organic Farming Research Foundation connects you with a community of professionals and enthusiasts. These organizations offer resources such as newsletters, research updates, and exclusive access to events. Attending gardening and horticulture conferences provides opportunities to learn about the latest research and innovations. Conferences often feature workshops, panel discussions, and exhibitions, offering a wealth of information in a short period. Participating in regional gardening expos and trade shows also allows you to see new products, tools, and techniques that can enhance your gardening efforts.

Continuing education and advanced courses are essential for any gardener looking to deepen their knowledge and skills. Whether through local extension programs, online courses, or professional associations, there are numerous opportunities to learn and grow. Engaging with these resources not only enhances your gardening expertise but also connects you with a broader community of passionate gardeners.

CONCLUSION

As the sun sets on our journey through "The Grinning Gardener's Handbook Volume 1," I hope you find yourself not just better informed, but deeply inspired. Our aim was to provide a comprehensive guide to growing organic fruits and vegetables, tailored to different climates and seasons. Gardening is more than a hobby; it's a way to connect with nature, nourish your body, and find peace in the simple act of nurturing life.

We've walked through the fundamental principles of organic gardening, emphasizing the importance of soil health, composting, and natural fertilizers. We've explored the intricacies of planning your garden, from choosing the right location to designing efficient layouts and understanding the nuances of microclimates. Each chapter provided detailed guidance on growing a variety of plants, from leafy greens to nightshades and berries, ensuring that you have the tools you need to cultivate a bountiful harvest.

You've learned about climate-specific gardening strategies, whether you're dealing with cold, hot, humid, or coastal environments. We've discussed soil and water management techniques to enhance plant health and productivity. Pest and disease control methods were explored with a focus on sustainable and eco-friendly practices, ensuring that your garden thrives without harming the environment.

In our journey, we also delved into advanced techniques like grafting, soil blocking, and vertical gardening, offering innovative solutions for maximizing space and improving plant health. We highlighted the significance of sustainable practices, such as water conservation and organic weed management, to create a garden that supports both your needs and the planet's.

Key takeaways from this book include the importance of understanding your garden's unique conditions and tailoring your practices accordingly. Soil health is the foundation of a thriving garden and managing it with organic matter and proper pH levels is crucial. Watering techniques, pest control, and crop rotation are essential for maintaining plant health and productivity. Advanced techniques like grafting and vertical gardening can enhance your garden's potential, while sustainable practices ensure its long-term viability.

Now, it's time to take what you've learned and put it into practice. Start by assessing your garden's current state and identifying areas for improvement. Experiment with different plants and techniques, and don't be afraid to make mistakes. Gardening is a continuous learning process, and each season brings new challenges and opportunities. Share your successes and challenges with fellow gardeners and contribute to a growing community of individuals committed to sustainable and organic gardening.

Remember, every garden tells a story. Yours is a story of growth, discovery, and transformation. As you tend to your plants, you're not just cultivating a garden; you're cultivating a space of joy, nourishment, and connection. May your garden flourish with vibrant colors, rich flavors, and the gentle hum of nature. And may you find in it the same peace and fulfillment that I have found in my own.

Thank you for allowing me to guide you on this journey. Happy gardening, and may your hands always be as green as your heart.

Warm Regards,

The Grinning Gardener

REFERENCES

- Britannica. (n.d.). Organic farming. In *Encyclopedia Britannica*. https://www.britannica.com/topic/organic-farming
- The Old Farmer's Almanac. (n.d.). How to test your garden soil (And 3 DIY tests). https://www.almanac.com/content/3-simple-diy-soil-tests
- U.S. Environmental Protection Agency. (n.d.). Composting at home. https://www.epa.gov/recycle/composting-home
- EOS Data Analytics. (n.d.). Organic fertilizers: Pros and cons, types, and role in farming. https://eos.com/blog/organic-fertilizers/#:
- SummerWinds Nursery. (n.d.). A how-to guide to mapping sun exposure in your garden. https://www.summerwindsnursery.com/az/inspire/blog/guide-to-mapping-garden-sun-exposure/
- Colorado State University Extension. (n.d.). Choosing a soil amendment (Fact Sheet No. 7.235). https://extension.colostate.edu/topic-areas/yard-garden/choosing-a-soil-amendment/
- U.S. Department of Energy. (n.d.). Landscaping for windbreaks. https://www.energy.gov/energysaver/landscaping-windbreaks#:
- Bayer Crop Science. (n.d.). Benefits and management of crop rotation. https://www.cropscience.bayer.us/articles/bayer/benefits-management-crop-rotation
- Oregon State University Extension. (n.d.). These cold-hardy vegetables may stick it out through winter. https://extension.oregonstate.edu/news/these-cold-hardy-vegetables-may-stick-it-out-through-winter#:
- Garden Design. (n.d.). Top 20 drought-tolerant plants for a waterwise landscape. https://www.gardendesign.com/plants/drought-tolerant.html
- Purdue University Extension. (n.d.). Disease resistant

- annuals and perennials in the landscape. https://www.extension.purdue.edu/extmedia/bp/id-414-w.pdf
- The Spruce. (n.d.). 24 types of salt-tolerant plants for beach and roadside landscaping. https://www.thespruce.com/salt-tolerant-plants-for-beach-and-roadside-landscaping-4767375
- North Dakota State University Agriculture. (n.d.). From garden to table: Leafy greens! https://www.ndsu.edu/agriculture/extension/publications/garden-table-leafy-greens#:
- Roots and Refuge. (n.d.). Organic garden pest control. https://rootsandrefuge.com/organic-garden-pest-control/
- University of Maryland Extension. (n.d.). Blossom end rot on vegetables. https://extension.umd.edu/resource/blossom-end-rot-vegetables
- Harris, S. L. (n.d.). Tips for making a cucumber trellis. https://stacylynharris.com/tips-for-using-garden-trellis/#:
- Pennsylvania State University Extension. (n.d.). Managing soil health: Concepts and practices. https://extension.psu.edu/managing-soil-health-concepts-and-practices
- Savvy Gardening. (n.d.). Blueberry fertilizer: How and when to feed blueberries. https://savvygardening.com/blueberry-fertilizer/
- Food Gardening Network. (n.d.). Growing zones for watermelon. https://foodgardening.mequoda.com/articles/growing-zones-for-watermelon/
- University of California Agriculture and Natural Resources. (n.d.). Grape pest management guidelines. https://ipm.ucanr.edu/agriculture/grape/
- The Spruce. (n.d.). How to test soil pH with and without a kit. https://www.thespruce.com/how-to-test-soil-acidity-alkalinity-without-a-test-kit-1388584
- Colorado State University Extension. (n.d.). Drip irrigation for home gardens (Fact Sheet No. 4.702). https://extension.colostate.edu/topic-areas/yard-garden/drip-irrigation-home-gardens-4-702/
- Texas A&M University. (n.d.). Mulches for water conservation. https://aggie-hort.tamu.edu/archives/parsons/drought/mulches.html

REFERENCES 155

- University of Minnesota Extension. (n.d.). Watering the vegetable garden. https://extension.umn.edu/how/watering-vegetable-garden#:~:text=Quick%20-facts,once%20a%20week%20is%20fine
- Growing Spaces. (n.d.). Ultimate guide to organic integrated pest management. https://growingspaces.com/integrated-pest-management/
- HowStuffWorks. (n.d.). 15 homemade organic gardening sprays that actually work. https://home.howstuffworks.com/green-living/homemade-organic-gardening-sprays.htm
- The Old Farmer's Almanac. (n.d.). Beneficial insects in the garden. https://www.almanac.com/beneficial-insects-garden
- Texas A&M Plant Disease Handbook. (n.d.). Non-chemical control of plant diseases in the home garden. https://plantdiseasehandbook.tamu.edu/problems-treatments/methods-and-materials/non-chemical-control-of-plant-diseases-in-the-home-garden/
- Mississippi State University Extension. (n.d.). Basic grafting techniques. http://extension.msstate.edu/publications/basic-grafting-techniques-0#:
- Johnny's Selected Seeds. (n.d.). Soil blocking: A better way to start seedlings. https://www.johnnyseeds.com/growers-library/methods-tools-supplies/seed-starting-transplanting/soil-blocking-seed-starting.html#:
- Whole Made Homestead. (n.d.). Vertical gardening for small spaces. https://wholemadehomestead.com/vertical-gardening-for-small-spaces/
- GrowVeg. (n.d.). Plan your garden to create perfect microclimates. https://www.growveg.com/guides/plan-your-garden-to-create-perfect-microclimates/
- Oregon State University Extension. (n.d.). Rainwater harvesting for use in the garden. https://extension.oregonstate.edu/catalog/pub/em-9101-harvesting-rainwater-use-garden
- Real Simple. (n.d.). 40 drought-tolerant plants that will improve your home's landscape. https://www.realsimple.com/home-organizing/gardening/outdoor/drought-tolerant-plants

- West Virginia University Organic Farming Research. (n.d.). Organic weed management. https://organic.wvu.edu/files/d/acab373b-6858-4a19-88b6-a1e142f030f0/organic-weed-management.pdf
- U.S. Department of Agriculture. (n.d.). Cover crops and crop rotation. https://www.usda.gov/peoples-garden/soil-health/cover-crops-crop-rotation#:
- University of Nebraska–Lincoln Extension. (n.d.). When to harvest fruits and vegetables. https://extensionpublications.unl.edu/assets/html/g2089/build/g2089.htm
- Hoss Tools. (n.d.). Essential supplies for efficient crop harvesting. https://growhoss.com/collections/harvesting-supplies?srsltid=AfmBOoo5Flzm6PenTHuJ7suZnWpwUy4uXuyAexazlYDA58YoJI8liPo8
- Michigan State University Extension. (n.d.). Storing root vegetables. https://www.canr.msu.edu/news/storing_root_vegetables
- Pennsylvania State University Extension. (n.d.). Preserving greens. https://extension.psu.edu/preserving-greens
- University of Maryland Extension. (n.d.). Nutrient deficiency of vegetable plants. https://extension.umd.edu/resource/nutrient-deficiency-vegetable-plants
- North Carolina State University Extension. (n.d.). Dealing with drought. https://gardening.ces.ncsu.edu/weather-2-2/dealing-with-drought/#:
- Iowa State University Extension and Outreach. (n.d.). Testing and improving soil drainage. https://yardandgarden.extension.iastate.edu/how-to/testing-and-improving-soil-drainage
- Missouri Botanical Garden. (n.d.). Overwatering. https://www.missouribotanicalgarden.org/gardens-gardening/your-garden/help-for-the-home-gardener/advice-tips-resources/insects-pests-and-problems/environmental/overwatering
- A Way to Garden. (n.d.). Organic vegetable gardening success stories with Joe Lamp'l. https://awaytogarden.com/organic-vegetable-gardening-success-stories-with-joe-lampl/

REFERENCES

- Greenberg, P. (n.d.). Community gardens: How U.S. cities are putting them to use. https://www.paulgreenberg.org/community-gardens-us-cities/
- Feedspot. (2024). 70 best organic gardening blogs and websites in 2024. https://gardening.feedspot.com/organic_gardening_blogs/
- eXtension. (n.d.). Find cooperative extension in your state. https://extension.org/find-cooperative-extension-in-your-state/

AUTHOR BIO

Kent Jameson grew up in a quaint farm town in Iowa, where he developed a deep appreciation for the simplicity of rural life. In 1994, he earned a Bachelor of Science degree in Family and Consumer Sciences Journalism from Iowa State University, laying the foundation for a life dedicated to exploring the intersection of family, health, and everyday issues that confront people.

Passionate about natural health, alternative medicines, and sustainable living, Kent's writing focuses on issues that directly affect families and consumers, offering thoughtful insights into how people can live healthier, more balanced lives in today's fast-paced world. Whether he's exploring the benefits of organic gardening, promoting holistic wellness practices, or discussing the challenges of modern life, Kent's work is always grounded in practical, real-world experience.

When he's not writing or tending to his garden, Kent enjoys spending time with his two sons, often cheering them on from the sidelines as they play basketball. Currently residing in Phoenix, Arizona, he continues to live by the values of simplicity and wellness that have guided him throughout his life and career.

Made in United States
Cleveland, OH
30 October 2025